Andrew Cuomo was supposed to be finished. After resigning in disgrace—accused by at least 11 women of sexual harassment and facing near-certain impeachment—New York's three-term governor vanished from public view. Now, in 2025, he's back. Cuomo is leading the polls in the New York City mayoral race, poised to reclaim power and write his own second act.

This new edition of *The Prince* unpacks Cuomo's long, bruising reign as governor and the forces that have enabled his climb back toward the spotlight. Barkan traces how Cuomo, once hailed as a pandemic hero, presided over a staggering public health failure—manipulating data, sending infected patients back into nursing homes, and pocketing a $5 million book deal for his self-mythologizing memoir. Cuomo, Return of the Dark Prince is a portrait of a man who refuses to go away—and a city that might just let him back in.

CUOMO

CUOMO

RETURN OF THE DARK PRINCE

ROSS BARKAN

O/R

OR Books

New York · London

Published by OR Books, New York and London
Visit our website at www.orbooks.com

All rights information: rights@orbooks.com

First published as *The Prince* 2021
First printing of this second edition, 2025

The manufacturer's authorised representative in the EU for product safety is Authorised Rep Compliance Ltd, 71 Lower Baggot Street, Dublin D02 P593 Ireland (www.arccompliance.com)

Typeset by Lapiz Digital. Printed by BookMobile, USA, and CPI, UK.

paperback ISBN 978-1-68219-442-3 • ebook ISBN 978-1-68219-445-4

For Vanessa, and my mother and father

CONTENTS

PREFACE
TO THE SECOND EDITION

Andrew Cuomo was back. Thundering from the podium in a union hall at the start of March, he warned of chaos and cataclysm. "We are here because we love New York and we know New York City is in trouble," he said. "You feel it when you walk down the street and you see the mentally ill homeless people. You feel it when you walk down into the subway and you feel the anxiety rise up in your chest. You hear it when you hear the scream of the police sirens."

And so the 2025 New York City mayoral race had begun in earnest. Cuomo—thinner, grayer, his wide face etched with deeper wrinkles—was plainly pleased. He led in all the polls. He was about to gobble up a bevy of labor endorsements. He was on the verge of becoming a political titan again and, more crucially for himself, forcibly rewriting his own obituary. For he had, three and a half years earlier, resigned in disgrace, credibly accused of sexually harassing at least 11 women. He had resigned only because the New York State Assembly was readying to impeach him and the State Senate, dominated by Democrats who wanted Cuomo gone, had the votes to convict. He had shuffled off into the shadows, to be replaced by a lieutenant governor he had, for many years, never taken seriously. All he could do was stew and begin plotting anew. Like another transactional, ego-mad, and savagely ambitious child of a Queens power broker, Cuomo was not going to let go. He wasn't going to practice law in the private sector, head up a nonprofit, or devote himself to charitable endeavors.

He was, like Donald Trump, going to try to reclaim power again, one way or another.

Before plunging into the 2025 mayoral race, Cuomo pondered a comeback bid in 2022. His one-time lackey, Kathy Hochul, was now governor. She was New York's first female governor and she wasn't overwhelmingly popular. Cuomo sniffed blood. But as the race drew closer, it was apparent that running so soon after scandal wasn't the wisest idea. Hochul was more potent than he had originally thought. She was raising gobs of money, as he once did, and barnstorming around the state. She wasn't going to bend the knee to him. If there was going to be a statewide Democratic primary between a sitting governor and a former governor, it would bruise him badly. He slunk back to the shadows.

It wasn't as if the 2025 race was any more promising. Eric Adams was the sitting mayor and he was, if nothing else, a brawler. A former police captain from a neighborhood in Queens not far from where Cuomo grew up—Adams was a child of the working-class, while Cuomo's father, Mario, was a star attorney who would end up governor—Adams had, in 2022, much going for him. Black and Latino Democrats strongly supported him, along with large labor unions and the city's business elite. With crime still elevated in the aftermath of the pandemic, Adams' tough talk held genuine appeal. He was a political chameleon with something for everyone. Michael Bloomberg, the billionaire three-term mayor, was an Adams supporter, as was Bill de Blasio, the progressive Democratic mayor and Bloomberg's successor. Adams, as mayor, was playing with an exceptionally strong hand.

But Adams, who once declared himself the face of the Democratic Party, would not stay dominant for long. He was deeply incompetent, stuffing his administration with patronage hires, and he barely prioritized governing. There were few memorable or significant policy initiatives to come out of City Hall. He preferred to cut ribbons during the day and club at night. New Yorkers rapidly soured on him as corruption clouds swirled around his administration. Finally, in September 2024, the Joe Biden-appointed U.S. Attorney for the Southern District, Damian Williams, indicted Adams on corruption charges. Already unpopular, his chances for re-election took an even greater hit. Adams did have one trump card to play, pun intended—the future president of the United States, who was also the past president, could pardon him.

Trump liked that Adams had fulminated against the Biden administration for the migrant influx into New York City. Adams, a couple of years earlier, had predicted that the surge of migrants, many of them from Venezuela, would "destroy" New

York. He blamed Democrats for their lax immigration policies. Republicans applauded. Once the indictment came, Adams began to cozy up to Trump—they were two outer borough boys who believed they were being persecuted by a Democrat-run Justice Department. When Trump won in November, Adams was effectively saved. The only question was how and when the charges would disappear. Rather than issue a blanket pardon, Trump took the path of least resistance: allowing his own Justice Department to abandon the case. The acting U.S. Attorney of the Southern District and lawyers within the Justice Department were outraged. It didn't matter that they resigned; Trump was in charge, and the case was dead. Adams was not heading to trial or prison.

Though he was free, the mayor's political standing continued to erode. Democrats in New York were fed up with him and it was increasingly clear he wasn't going to win the primary. A large field of candidates, including the sitting city comptroller, Brad Lander, and a popular democratic socialist assemblyman named Zohran Mamdani, had taken shape to oust the sitting mayor. And Cuomo relished it all. For many months, he had been rumored to run. His fiery spokesman, Richard Azzopardi, had been gleefully jousting with the press. His closest aide—and, at one time, the most powerful woman in New York—Melissa DeRosa had been strategizing openly about what a Cuomo mayoral campaign might look like. Cuomo had been initially wary of running against Adams because he wanted to court the Black voters who made up the mayor's political base.

As Adams grew less popular, that became easier to do. Orthodox Jews, another pillar of the Adams coalition, seemed possible to win over. The labor unions and billionaire real estate developers who had reflexively backed Cuomo's gubernatorial campaigns were receptive, at least, to the inevitability of a Cuomo comeback. He was the devil they knew.

One way to understand Cuomo is Trump with intellect and discipline. Cuomo is a serious person. His campaign for mayor could be built around tangible accomplishments, like the rehab of LaGuardia Airport and the opening of Moynihan Station in Manhattan. He had more than a decade of executive experience to tout to an electorate that was desperate for a leader after three years of farce under Adams. The city, meanwhile, had shifted gradually to the right, with concerns about crime and immigration making a belligerent centrist like Cuomo more appealing. With many of the Democrats in the primary running center-left or leftist campaigns, Cuomo could seize the middle and wait. His own campaign was dreadnought-like, blasting through the municipal waters, ignoring all in its wake. He wasn't going to shake many hands or talk to too many reporters. He was going to run out the clock.

Could he? That was the operative question of the winter and spring. Past mayoral races had obvious frontrunners, but none as overwhelming as Cuomo. His sexual harassment scandals didn't seem to matter, nor did his catastrophic failures during Covid. As the other candidates strained in his shadow, Cuomo simply barreled forward. He neared 40% in the polls, and in ranked-choice voting simulations—in New York, voters could rank up to five candidates in the primary—he plainly came out ahead. It was his race to lose.

A second question became: why *not* choose Cuomo? Time had passed and his scandals no longer seemed pressing. The #MeToo movement had lost steam. New Yorkers were fine with flawed leaders as long as they led. And there was something comforting in having a bully represent them. Trump wanted to fight, so let New York have its own Queens boy to throw a few meaty punches back at him.

I do not, in this book, seek to tell you how to vote. Your choice of candidate is up to you. What I offer, instead, is an exploration of Cuomo's eleven-year reign as governor, one that featured both lasting accomplishments and debilitating failures. Above all else, I seek to bring you facts and eviscerate myths. Once you see clearly, you can make your own decisions. It's important, at least, to understand who Andrew Mark Cuomo is and what he has done. You will learn that here. I can promise that.

Cuomo is the governor who dispatched Covid patients back to nursing homes, fueling the spread of the virus there. He is the governor who actively manipulated public data to show an artificially lower Covid death toll in those nursing homes. He is the governor who, as the pandemic raged, accepted a $5 million book advance to write on his own alleged heroics. He is the governor who, like Trump and other Republicans, initially downplayed the threat of Covid and compared it to the flu. He is the governor who delayed locking down New York as the virus spread because his political rival, Mayor Bill de Blasio, called for a shutdown order first. He is the governor who sought drastic Medicaid cuts during this pandemic; he is the governor who was always comfortable imposing austerity on the city's public university system. He is the governor who closed enough hospitals, in the years prior to Covid, that overcrowding and mass death, come 2020, could be the only result.

He is the governor, too, who undercut Democrats in New York for a decade. He is the governor who let the subway system deteriorate. He is the governor who tolerated shocking amounts of corruption in his own government.

The story of the pandemic in New York cannot be told without Andrew Cuomo. And the story of New York itself, in the twenty-first century, is at least partially the story of this imperial governor. We live in an era of strongmen, of ever greater flirtations with authoritarianism. Few governors, at their height, wielded more power and influence than Cuomo. Few, in any state, knew what it was to impose their will on millions. Cuomo could, at one time, shut down the world's largest subway system on a whim. He could force America's largest city to start paying the rent of privately-run schools. He could compel prisoners to produce thousands of gallons of hand sanitizer.

Cuomo as mayor would not quite have the same authority. New York City is, in many ways, a creature of New York State government. The governor and legislature could constrain him. But Mayor Cuomo would be formidable. He would command the nation's largest police force. He would oversee the nation's largest school system. There would be much for him to do. And he won't forget those who stood against him. He holds deeper grudges than Trump and he's far more competent. Unlike Trump, transactions and dealmaking only go so far; de Blasio, for example, strained for years to accommodate Cuomo, significantly aiding one of his re-election bids. It didn't matter. Cuomo perceived a threat and sought to stamp it out. Those who now want to rehabilitate Cuomo—who are prepared to usher him into City Hall—don't quite understand what it is that's in front of them. Cuomo won't rest until revenge is meted out. "Love endures by a bond which men, being scoundrels, may break whenever it serves their advantage to do so; but fear is supported by the dread of pain, which is ever present," Niccolo Machiavelli once wrote. These are words Cuomo, implicitly and explicitly, has long lived by. He would like worship and adulation, but that is only so interesting to him. He is not one to press flesh or mug for cameras. He understands that, in politics, the "dread of pain" is ever-present and that the smartest operators—and certainly the most cutthroat—know how to exploit it.

Here, once more, comes Cuomo. He is never to be underestimated.

—April 2025

INTRODUCTION

On a warm day just before the start of summer, Governor Andrew Cuomo addressed the people of New York State and the nation for the 111th consecutive day. He was alone this time, not confining himself to a room with journalists or lecturing in front of PowerPoint slides. There were no celebrities flanking him. In a pale tie and dark suit, a photograph of his three daughters framed just to his right, Cuomo spoke with the emotion of a man who had witnessed catastrophe but conquered it completely.

"Over the past three months we have done the impossible," Cuomo said. "We are controlling the virus better than any state in the country and any nation in the globe. I am so incredibly proud of what we all did together and as a community. We reopened the economy and we saved lives—because it was never a choice between one or the other. It was always right to do both."

The governor, speaking behind his desk on live television, did not take questions. He didn't have to. Among most of those watching—the operatives, the aides, the reporters, the enormous, reverential public—there was the feeling of a job well done, a crisis now in retreat. On that Friday, with the temperature nearing 90 degrees in the state capital of Albany, the number of people hospitalized was 1,284, compared to the more than 18,000 at the peak of the outbreak. "I thought about it every day as climbing a mountain. The Mount Everest of social challenges," Cuomo said.

The address was relatively brief, clocking in at about nine minutes and fifteen seconds, and it closed with a somber yet celebratory video slideshow overlaid with narration from the governor himself. Images flashed across the screen: Cuomo, sepia-toned, with his top aide, Melissa DeRosa. Cuomo, huddled with tough men in camouflage. A whiteboard scrawled with facts about the virus. A boy removing one mask to display another mask, a message in marker combining on each: *We Are All NY Tough.*

Men and women appeared in masks. Others cheered from rooftops and balconies. "We have the lowest rate of transmission," came Cuomo's voice, the string music rising. "The phased reopening is working. Stay the course."

Nowhere in the video came the death toll. This wasn't a surprise. It was a day for valedictions, for aspiration and ultimately relief. The dreaded virus was raging elsewhere. It was done, it seemed, with New York. For Cuomo, once a politician who could spend weeks without addressing a single reporter, it was a special kind of validation, the type he had been seeking in a lonely decade, from one of the nation's most powerful perches.

Through all the triumphs, the failures, and the late-night rage channeled across telephone lines, Cuomo seemed to be a man cursed to govern in his father's shadow, more feared than loved. He rarely shook hands at parades or rode the subway with the average commuter. Until 2020, he was not famous in any conventional sense, not in the currency of new media, never lodged too deeply in the consciousness of the state he had controlled since 2011.

Yet by June 19, the coronavirus briefings had drawn nearly 60 million online views, on par with the music videos of mid-level pop stars. Cuomo's favorability rating had ranged as high as 77 percent.

The 111th press briefing would be the last regular daily briefing of the coronavirus pandemic, Cuomo had declared earlier that week. Though he inevitably would need to address the public again. He had set or broken a record no one knew existed, appearing day after day on the television screens of a terrified public hungry for guidance. Donald Trump, another Queens native who had once been a Cuomo donor, was incapable of providing it in the White House, where he passed the days in a fugue of rage and idiocy.

Cuomo was the contrast, hurling bare facts at his viewers and sternly comforting them, like a father huddling his brood in the London Tube during the Blitz. He spoke of his elderly mother and his loving daughters, invited up Rosie Perez and Chris Rock, unveiled a wall of colorful cloth face masks, and once took a nasal swab test for all to see.

We had all been in this together. The journalists, tasked with covering the briefings typically staged in either New York City or Albany, reflected on what they had experienced, seated with Cuomo as he became a national phenomenon. Most of those who had covered the governor for a long period of time developed newfound appreciation in this period, praising him as columnists and pundits further removed from the Albany fray had done for months on end.

Deeming it a "remarkable run," the *New York Times'* Albany bureau chief, Jesse McKinley, wrote that he "thought the pleas for unity and understanding seemed genuine."

"It seemed telling, too, that he quoted famous thinkers— Lincoln, Maya Angelou—letting them lend him gravitas," McKinley continued. "His own truisms he sneaked into briefings by quoting a person who didn't exist, A. J. Parkinson, an inside joke and old trick of his father's, but also a tactic I found revealing: Here was a man who wanted to make maxims, but didn't necessarily want to be credited—or criticized—for trying to sound profound."

The *Times* journalist wondered in his piece, published on June 14, if a state that had seen more than 30,000 coronavirus deaths—by far the most in the United States of America, rivaling the death tolls of European nations—could claim any kind of success. But it was a question posed in the eighth paragraph, passed over quickly enough. "Definitive answers won't be known for years," McKinley wrote.

But that couldn't have been farther from the truth. The reckoning came far sooner than many anticipated, with a speed and fury that shocked sclerotic Albany.

One year after the virus first appeared in New York and Cuomo's press briefings made him wildly famous, the majority leader of the United States Senate, Chuck Schumer, and a vast number of New York's congressional delegation and state legislature were calling for Cuomo to resign. The State Assembly had launched an impeachment investigation. In the span of one calendar year, Cuomo had reached heights and depths that few politicians alive had ever known.

The genesis of his downfall was the release of a State Attorney General's report, in early 2021, that found his Department of Health had severely undercounted nursing home deaths. Shortly after, he berated a state lawmaker who had challenged him on the issue, drawing national headlines.

And then came another scandal, which would imperil the governor's career. At least six women accused Cuomo of sexual harassment. Several were former aides. One, Lindsey Boylan, said he forcibly kissed her. Another claimed he groped her in the Executive Mansion. A third, Charlotte Bennett, worked under Cuomo and alleged he made deeply inappropriate remarks to her, essentially propositioning her for sex.

The Cuomo administration attempted to tarnish the reputation of Boylan, a candidate for local office, circulating an open letter disclosing personnel complaints against her. This was a tactic they had long employed against those who challenged the boss—intimidate and smear, undercutting the complaint before it could gain traction. This time, though, it wouldn't work.

After denying most of the tawdrier allegations and attempting to have a law partner of one of his closest government allies oversee an investigation into them, Cuomo was forced to allow the State Attorney General, Letitia James, to conduct a probe.

The allegations made Cuomo, once again, the dominant national news story. The prestige media outlets and cable television networks that had elevated him in the earliest days of the pandemic were now scrutinizing him hourly, filling a void that had been left by the most scandalous politician in modern history, Trump.

After a moment of contrition, Cuomo would inevitably adopt Trump's posture: disingenuous martyrdom. "People know the difference between playing politics, bowing to cancel culture, and the truth," Cuomo bellowed during a March 12 press call. "I am not a part of the political club."

If Cuomo was not a part of the political club, the club simply could not exist. The son of a governor, the ex-husband of a Kennedy, and a Clinton-era cabinet official was nothing but a creature of elite Democratic politics. But the machine he was reared in—and the one he had come to dominate—was rejecting him. In his darkest hour, he parroted the unhinged rhetoric of the right-wing he had spent four years mocking and deriding. This was not a group of students swarming over mean tweets: this was the revolt of a political class that no longer had use for him.

The sexual harassment scandal could not be entirely decoupled from the pandemic. For months, Cuomo had intentionally downplayed the number of coronavirus deaths in nursing homes, refusing demands from elected officials, journalists, and advocates to produce a proper tally. James, the attorney general, released a report in January 2021 that found Cuomo's Department of Health had undercounted deaths in those facilities by as much as 50 percent.

Virtually overnight, the tally was revised, nearly doubling. But a revision wouldn't be enough, not with allegations swirling of a Nixonian cover-up. In February, the FBI launched a probe into the Cuomo administration, raising the kind of legal jeopardy Cuomo hadn't experienced since his closest aide, Joe Percoco, was sent to federal prison on bribery charges a few years earlier.

In the midst of the breaking scandal, Cuomo was revealed to be, for the wider world, what he had always been: exceedingly arrogant, vengeful, and megalomaniacal, the kind of boss who demanded women in his office wear high heels and lowly aides struggle in Darwinian competitions for his amusement. It was a culture that favored dominance over competence. It was a culture, deeply insular and self-serving, that was designed to place Cuomo at its center.

It was this culture, ultimately, that had given New York a pandemic response that was incapable of effectively mitigating catastrophe in any meaningful way. As COVID-19 raged across America, infecting big cities and small towns alike, and bedeviling both Democrats and Republicans, there was the inarguable body count: around 50,000 dead in New York, far more than in most any other state in the country.

By the close of 2020, New York's death rate—like those of a number of American states—had easily surpassed that of Spain and Italy's, two of the worst coronavirus hotspots in Europe. Only neighboring New Jersey, so closely tied to New York City, had a higher death rate. Jay Inslee, the governor of Washington

State and a failed presidential contender, garnered little fame for holding down the death rate in his state to 35 per 100,000 people, even though Washington was the original coronavirus epicenter in America. New York, meanwhile, had seen 178 per 100,000 people die by December 2020.

There is a strong case to be made that the plaudits Cuomo won during the darkest days of the pandemic were wholly undeserved. There should have been no heights for Cuomo to fall from, no media-generated mythos to eventually obliterate. At the most crucial point for the preservation of life in the state he governed, Cuomo failed to prevent mass death on a scale never before seen. New York City's death toll alone surpassed 30,000, more than nine times the fatalities on September 11.

How much of this can be joined to the actions taken by Cuomo and his nemesis, New York City Mayor Bill de Blasio? There is no way to attribute a specific number. Trump spent the early months of 2020 downplaying, ignoring, or lying about coronavirus altogether, and failed to scale up an adequate national response. States were left to fend for themselves, federalism at its most dire. No discussion of Cuomo's leadership can ignore the federal failure. And even competent leaders, as evidenced in Europe, struggled with containing a virus that was so highly contagious, spreading through the most innocent of human interactions.

Those who spend enough time analyzing the Wonderland-quality of New York politics may come away with the mistaken impression that Cuomo and de Blasio were symmetrical combatants, sharing equal blame for New York's coronavirus carnage. But that's not right either. Though there is no way to tie individual deaths to one action or another, there is a clear record to suggest Cuomo's decision-making in late February and early March doomed New York to far more suffering than it should have experienced, particularly when leaders elsewhere tamped down on the initial spread of a virus that was then at its most deadly, and physicians and healthcare workers had little understanding of how to treat it best.

In the dark logic of the pandemic year, Cuomo won fabulous praise for being everything he wasn't: calm, decisive, and trafficking in the worlds of fact and reason. He shut down New York City far too late and, like Trump, dismissed the threat of coronavirus. He mismanaged nursing homes and covered up the true death count there. He gave hospitals and nursing homes sweeping legal immunity, outflanking Republicans in Washington who wanted to do the same, and farmed out critical decisions to the healthcare lobby. He failed to quickly release inmates from state prisons as the virus spread unchecked. He pursued, in the heart of the pandemic, deep and destabilizing cuts to social services and education.

Imagine, for a moment, Nero garnering critical acclaim for fiddling as Rome burned.

★ ★ ★

This book is a chronicling of the plague year in New York. The first two chapters, "Infection" and "Fear," timeline the spread of coronavirus in New York and America in grim detail, demonstrating how Cuomo misled the public and bumbled into catastrophe. All the while this fed a false reality, in which he was portrayed as a competent governor-hero, to a starry-eyed, compliant media.

Next, "Carnage" and "Tally" explore the consequences of the true reality—mass suffering and death. In the final chapter, "Austerity," I examine the decisions Cuomo made many years prior to the pandemic that led New York on this road to disaster.

Indeed, beyond Cuomo's failure during New York's most precarious hours, there is another story to be told—one of power. Cuomo has been governor of New York for more than a decade and has dreamed of surpassing his father, Mario, who governed for three full terms. Cuomo is, as of 2021, the second-longest tenured governor in America.

With New York's lack of term limits and loose campaign finance laws, there was little, until recently, to stop Cuomo from dominating New York indefinitely. He remains the state's most powerful governor since Nelson Rockefeller, who was one of the richest men in history. From New York springs those who inspire and torment the nation: the Roosevelts, the Rockefellers, the Trumps. Cuomo has been one of the most significant local political figures in the last half century, a man with all of Robert Moses's pharaonic ambition, longing to bend government to his will.

Cuomo's ascent, like any true prince's, could not have been possible without his father. The Cuomo name, to New York

Democrats, is not so different than what Kennedy once meant to the nation. There is no Andrew Cuomo without Mario Cuomo. And like the monarchs who once read, with great attention, Niccolò Machiavelli's 16th-century treatise, Cuomo long ago learned that to govern, it is often better to be feared than loved. He has been unafraid of humiliating and punishing rivals; until very recently, few Democrats dared challenge him in the open.

Cuomo's tragic failure to prevent so many deaths cannot be understood without untangling the decisions he made, in the seat of power, throughout the 2010s. A believer in austerity governance, he shuttered hospitals that could have treated patients in the outer reaches of New York City as the coronavirus first struck. He sought, over the decade prior to the pandemic and during it, to cut funding to the remaining public hospitals, following through on long-held aims to curtail healthcare spending. His quest to placate wealthier voters led to onerous property tax caps that constrained municipal and social services. His close ties to the real estate industry meant that many more renters were vulnerable to the predatory whims of landlords, as he refused, again and again, to strengthen tenant laws for much of his tenure. He never even entertained the widespread call for canceling rent as the pandemic raged and hundreds of thousands of people lost their jobs.

For much of the time he held office, this hero of anti-Trump liberals helped Republicans hold the majority in the New York State Senate. Indeed, he participated in the creation of the Independent Democratic Conference, a breakaway group of conservative Democrats who propped up Republicans from 2013 through 2018. Like his father, Mario, another icon of sections of the left, he distrusted the progressive wing of his party. But unlike the apparently squeaky clean Mario, a corruption investigation sent Cuomo junior's closest aide to prison and nearly ensnared him too.

To a dwindling number of Democrats Cuomo is still a hero, representing all that a leader should be. It is important to remember that Robert Moses, the master builder of New York who often pursued a destructive and discriminatory reimagining of the city in the 20th century, was once a local idol, his every act celebrated by an adoring press. It would take decades, and the dogged reporting of Robert Caro and others, to tell a story that reflected the reality of those who suffered the indignity and the terror of their neighborhoods torn asunder by Moses' megalomania.

History will reckon with Cuomo too. Journalists, historians, and the many eyewitnesses to 2020 and 2021 will begin to produce honest and thorough accounts of what happened in this most tragic time. As a native New York City journalist myself, I have written about Cuomo since his first term. This book is based on original reporting I conducted throughout the early months of COVID-19 as well as more recent interviews and research. I am also indebted to the many strong journalists who, swimming against a strong tide to do so, attempted to debunk Cuomo's false narrative of triumph. Select journalists at outlets like Gothamist, ProPublica, the Albany *Times Union*, the *New York Times*, the *New York Post*, the *Wall Street Journal*, the Associated Press, the *Guardian,* and *Politico*, among others, were invaluable as I researched this book.

Cuomo will not always have the aid of his bully pulpit and press briefings to defend himself, to shape reality as he believes it should be. He will not always have his favored cable television show hosts and pundits. Into this uncertain future, once more, a colossus of New York has met a public more immune to charms and mythmaking.

Cuomo's father could never outlast all of his rivals. Through pandemic and scandal and the revolt of his party's left flank, Cuomo still hopes to be different. At the time of writing in March 2021, instead of winding down his career, as any other politician in his imperiled position would, he is maniacally forging on—and hoping, just like the old days, his opposition crumbles away. It will be a grave injustice if this happens. Cuomo never deserved to be fawned over in the local and national media. His heroism was built on lies. We can only hope, in time, the truth of 2020 and 2021 is understood on a mass scale—and lessons are learned for the next plague year.

INFECTION

On the last day of the decade, China announced a strange new cluster of pneumonia cases. Those who had fallen ill had all been linked to the Huanan Seafood Wholesale Market in Wuhan, Hubei Province. By January 3, a total of 44 patients with this pneumonia had been reported to the World Health Organization by the national authorities in China. Of the 44 cases reported, 11 were severely ill, while the remaining 33 patients were in stable condition.[1] Days later, Chinese health authorities confirmed that this cluster of cases was associated with something called the novel coronavirus, 2019-nCoV.

It was news, thousands of miles away, that hardly made a ripple. Americans were transfixed, as always, by the spectacle of President Donald Trump, who had just been impeached. The Democrat-controlled House of Representatives had alleged Trump withheld military aid and an invitation to the White House to Ukrainian president Volodymyr Zelensky in order to influence Ukraine to announce an investigation into Joe Biden, the former vice president and one of the top Democrats seeking to challenge Trump in 2020. A trial in the Republican-controlled Senate was scheduled for February, and many liberal

Americans desperately hoped Trump, somehow, could be driven from office.

On January 7, when Chinese health authorities officially confirmed the existence of COVID-19, Washington, DC was aflutter with the news that John Bolton, Trump's hawkish former national security advisor, could testify if subpoenaed at the Senate trial. Beyond impeachment, there were fears America could be on the brink of war with Iran after US forces, in a wanton act of aggression, assassinated Qassem Soleimani, a top Iranian general. That Wednesday, Iran had struck back, firing a series of ballistic missiles at two military bases in Iraq housing American troops.

It was Iran's most direct assault on America since the 1979 seizing of the US Embassy. The day before, a massive stampede broke out at Soleimani's funeral, killing at least 56 and injuring more than 200, according to Iranian news reports.

Beyond such international crises and the looming reality of America's first impeachment trial in more than 20 years, there was a Democratic primary for president being waged. This time, the contest would be far more unwieldy, with more than a dozen candidates competing for the opportunity to defeat Trump— assuming he survived February. Many of the candidates were clustered in Iowa, hoping to repeat Barack Obama's path to the White House with a surprise victory there. Appearing at a fundraiser in New York City, Biden warned the next 10 months on the campaign trail would be a "long slog." Though it will be an "ugly race," Biden said, "it has to be run."[2]

On the same January day that Biden trekked to Manhattan to raise cash from wealthy donors who still held out hope he could triumph over Bernie Sanders, the left's top candidate, Governor Andrew Cuomo arrived nearby to make a significant announcement. Entering his tenth year in the governor's mansion, Cuomo enjoyed little more than flexing government's largest, most visible muscle: infrastructure.

In near-complete control of a budget that had, as of 2019, neared $180 billion,[3] Cuomo could funnel enormous amounts of public money into the kind of immense construction projects that would long outlast him. So, thrilled to cut the ribbon on the first span of a relatively minor bridge connecting the boroughs of Brooklyn and Queens a few years earlier, Cuomo drove across in a 1932 Packard that belonged to Franklin Delano Roosevelt. The dazzling, multicolored LED light show set to music that accompanied the bridge's opening cost New York State more than $200 million alone.[4]

But in January Cuomo's attention had turned to Penn Station. Eight new tracks would be added to the dismal transit hub, which sat beneath Madison Square Garden in Midtown Manhattan. The aim, Cuomo said in a speech, would be to alleviate congestion at an underground train station serving large swaths of commuters from neighboring suburbs. By the end of the year, a new train hall was slated to open across the street in the old James A. Farley Post Office Building.

"There is no alternative, because paralysis is a death sentence. Inertia is a death sentence. If we do nothing, the world passes us by," Cuomo said.[5]

Cuomo had hoped to cultivate this image above all others, of a man of action forcing feckless bureaucracy to do what it should. Roosevelt was one model. Lyndon B. Johnson was another. In a fawning opinion piece that undoubtedly made Cuomo smile, a New York City councilman once compared Cuomo to the president who gave America Medicare, Medicaid, and sweeping civil rights legislation.[6]

By the start of the new year, though, Cuomo was not quite Johnson in New York. He had twice defeated Republicans in elections that weren't particularly close, but New York was a largely Democratic state and no pundit gave him significant credit for brushing them away. He had repelled two primary challenges as well, but neither candidate had close to the resources and name recognition he possessed.

There had been no serious, sustained buzz around him seeking the presidency in 2020. This didn't seem to particularly bother Cuomo, who hated traveling outside the state, but there was the nagging realization that he would never be as beloved as his father, who governed New York for much of the 1980s and early 1990s. Cuomo the younger was grimmer, more plodding, devoid of such charisma and gravitas. His father's 1984 speech at the Democratic National Convention was still remembered as one of the best ever. The hardiest of politico pros could not recall what exactly the son had said in his own speech at the 2016 convention.

The numbers backed this up. In a November 2019 Siena College poll, Cuomo's approval and favorability ratings were distressing. Both had sunk underwater. His favorability rating, a measure of sheer likability, stood at 44 percent, with 49 percent of voters finding him unfavorable. His job approval rating was worse: 35 rated it positive, while a shocking 65 percent judged him negatively.[7] None of this meant Cuomo could be easily defeated when he inevitably ran again in 2022—New York has no term limits for state officials—but it called into question what his purpose would be. He was not a leader of the Democratic Party nationally and he was not particularly embraced by the voters of his own state. The problem wasn't just Republicans and independents, who could always judge harshly a governor who had hung around so long. "After two months in slightly positive territory, Cuomo's favorability has fallen back into negative territory, and it's largely because of Democrats," said Steve Greenberg, Siena College's pollster, in November 2019. "His favorability rating among Democrats is now 59–34 percent, down from 68–29 percent last month."

The year ahead, for Cuomo, wasn't particularly promising. An emboldened state legislature, now entirely controlled by Democrats for the first time in a decade, could begin to act without his input, forcing bills to his desk that he would be pressured to sign. And beyond New York, Cuomo was simply not the most famous or relevant Democrat. Chuck Schumer, New York's senior senator, could finally get his opportunity to become majority leader after the fall elections. Michael Bloomberg, the billionaire former mayor of New York City, was running for president.

Cuomo had always reveled in crises, whether manmade or sprung from nature. In the aftermath of Hurricane Sandy in 2012, Cuomo donned his New York State windbreaker and toured the wreckage. He strode through subway tunnels for photo ops. Years later, he came across a car crash on a highway and cut a passenger out of his seatbelt.[8]

A deadly virus loomed and Cuomo sprung into action.

It was Ebola, and the year was 2014. Striking West Africa, the virus would end up killing more than 11,000 people, with a fatality rate of 40 percent. In the fall, a doctor returning from Guinea tested positive in New York, setting off a scramble to figure out who else might have been infected.

Cuomo and his counterpart in New Jersey, Chris Christie, ordered a mandatory 21-day quarantine of anyone returning from West Africa who had direct contact with Ebola patients. The policy drew sharp criticism from aid organizations, medical professionals, and even the Obama White House. A volunteer nurse with Doctors Without Borders was detained in New Jersey and forced into isolation despite testing negative for the virus. She worried about the fates of her colleagues.

"Will they be made to feel like criminals and prisoners?" she asked.[9] Cuomo defended the policy, joking that those forced into quarantine could read his newly-released memoir, which would sell less than 4,000 copies despite an advance of $783,000.[10]

The quarantine had made Cuomo appear tough and commanding, though it violated the known facts of Ebola. The virus was not so highly contagious; only those showing symptoms could spread it to someone else. There was no need to forcefully quarantine anyone testing negative. The Obama White House took particular umbrage with Cuomo and Christie's policy because they feared it would discourage doctors from traveling to West Africa to treat Ebola patients.

When Ebola failed to materialize as a threat in the United States, the controversy surrounding the Cuomo-Christie quarantine policy faded. By 2020, the national conversation had turned to the Democratic primary and the impeachment of Trump. COVID-19, the strange new virus, was rapidly spreading in China. But would it get here?

The answer, by mid-January, was yes.

In the months to come, Cuomo would claim the virus ambushed New York and an incompetent federal response hampered his state's ability to prepare. Some of this was accurate. But New York did not grapple with the first confirmed coronavirus cases in America. A 35-year-old man in a Seattle suburb had walked into an urgent-care clinic with a cough and a slight fever. He told doctors that he'd just returned from Wuhan, China.

The announcement was made on January 21.

★ ★ ★

Washington State's encounter with coronavirus would be instructive and is relevant to lay out before we move to New York's. Other states would be able to, in theory, learn from how

Washington tried to contain this new and very contagious virus. By the end of February, community transmission had been discovered, and King County would record the nation's first coronavirus fatality. By February 29, there were a total of six cases identified in the county.[11]

Though COVID-19 wasn't as well understood as it would be in the subsequent months of 2020, among epidemiologists, publicly and privately, it was regarded as inevitable that coronavirus would spread to other large cities, including New York. As early as February 25, Dr. Nancy Messonnier, the director of the Centers for Disease Control's National Center for Immunization and Respiratory Diseases, warned that community spread seemed imminent, and disruption to American communities could be significant.

"It is not a question of if coronavirus will spread through the United States," Messonnier said, "but a question of when and how many people will have severe illness."[12]

On a conference call with reporters, Messonnier laid out steps communities and individuals may have to take if spread of the virus picked up, including school and workplace closures, quarantines, and the canceling of mass gatherings. Local health officials in Washington State understood quickly that those getting sick didn't have to come from China. Community spread was underway and many more were likely infected.

"I think, like anything, what we're seeing is the tip of the iceberg," said Dr. Francis Riedo, an infectious disease expert in Seattle, at a news conference on February 29.[13] "We're seeing the most critically ill individuals. Usually that means there is a significant percentage of individuals with less severe illness floating around out there."

There was little time to delay. Ordering a shutdown on the scale of what Wuhan endured—a severe restriction of all travel into and out of the city—would be logistically impossible. Some Americans had been reading the news coming out of China but most were not aware of coronavirus posing any kind of true threat, since so few people had been noticeably infected. But the problem lay in what was coming: the exponential spread of a virus that could endanger tens of thousands of people in a matter of days.

In King County, public health officials urged the county executive, Dow Constantine, to shutter Seattle's schools. The public school system served the city's most vulnerable students and any kind of long-term closure would be debilitating, since many students relied on the schools for free breakfast and lunch. Remote learning would be a tremendous challenge and invite backlash.

Yet the schools wouldn't necessarily be closed in Seattle, because of fears that they would soon become hubs of viral transmission. Undoubtedly they could, experts believed, but, but it was just as important to shock the populace into taking coronavirus seriously. In 2019, Seattle closed schools for five days after a series of snowstorms and the Seattle Flu Study soon discovered that traffic in certain areas nearly disappeared, public-transit use decreased rapidly, and the transmission of influenza declined.

Constantine wanted to ensure epidemiologists were empowered to communicate with a nervous and confused public—and politicians wouldn't necessarily be the leading voices on the nightly news. On February 29, the day Governor Jay Inslee declared a state of emergency, three top health officials in Seattle and the State of Washington—Riedo, Dr. Jeff Duchin, and Dr. Kathy Lofy—played prominent roles at a news conference. Critically, Washington State politicians would cede important public communications about COVID-19 to people like Duchin, the top public health official for Seattle and King County.

Meanwhile, Constantine urged one of Washington's largest employers, Microsoft, to make most workers telecommute. Like shutting public schools, having the cooperation of Microsoft, such a prominent corporation, was viewed as crucial in any public health response. A few days later, Microsoft finalized a work-from-home policy and the workforce at the main campus would plunge from 40,000 to less than 5,000.[14]

On March 4, Constantine publicly called on all employers to allow employees to work from home. On that day, there were at least 31 confirmed cases of coronavirus in King County.[15]

Within a week, on March 10, Inslee restricted gatherings of more than 250 people, shutting down sporting events, concerts, and larger cultural events. On March 11, after much consternation—many officials worried about the repercussions of closing schools for the poorest students—it was announced all public schools would close the next day. By then, much of downtown Seattle had emptied out, with telecommuting taking effect and clear warnings from public health officials coming through daily.

The recitation of these rather dry facts is crucial for understanding what could have been done in America's largest city to prevent such an enormous amount of death. The most enlightened elected officials and scientists could not keep all people from dying from coronavirus, or even hold off a death toll in the thousands: in time, more than 3,000 people would die of COVID-19 in the state of Washington. But when a contagious virus is new and poorly understood by the general public, words and decisions are amplified. Every utterance from a powerful person about the threat can directly determine future behavior.

Some liberals have overwhelmingly digested this lesson with Donald Trump. A denier of climate change regularly at odds with empirical reality, Trump displayed no mastery of epidemiology and did not empower experts to lead the way. He hoped coronavirus would go away, in part because of fears—eventually realized—that an outbreak could derail the stock market in his reelection year. At a political rally on February 9, Trump declared that "by April, you know, in theory, when it gets a little warmer, [coronavirus] miraculously goes away."[16] Trump named Mike Pence, his slavishly devoted vice president, to lead the coronavirus response, not any official with a public health background.

Of course, in the early months, there were otherwise well-meaning public health officials who deeply misled the American public on how to take certain precautions. This was a failure that went beyond the Trump administration to a misguided notion that any recommendation of facial coverings could lead to a rush for supplies that would deprive healthcare workers, even if ordinary Americans could be advised to wear simple cloth coverings until more durable masks became widely available.

"The fact that people are wearing masks—number one, it's not helpful and number two, it's overly alarmist," said Isaac Bogoch, an infectious diseases doctor and professor at the University of Toronto, on January 29.[17] "If someone has a respiratory infection, masks are helpful at stopping spread. But if people are uninfected wearing a little flimsy mask, it is not going to significantly reduce their risk of acquiring this infection."

A month later, the US Surgeon General was even more blunt. "Seriously people—STOP BUYING MASKS! They are NOT effective in preventing general public from catching #Coronavirus, but if healthcare providers can't get them to care for sick patients, it puts them and our communities at risk!" he tweeted.[18]

In New York, at the end of February, the posture from the state's most powerful elected official was less reality-challenged than Trump's, but also far removed from what had been expressed in King County. On the same day Dr. Francis Riedo, the infectious disease expert in Seattle, warned that "what we're seeing is the tip of the iceberg," Andrew Cuomo compared preparing for coronavirus to forecasting a weather event.[19]

First, Cuomo emphasized the importance of building testing capacity for coronavirus in New York, and that the CDC had approved the state's test. "We can start testing immediately," he said, addressing reporters. His voice rising and his right index finger floating in the air, Cuomo then turned to the future of COVID-19.

"There are a number of trajectories, a number of forecasts with the coronavirus. It's like looking at the weather map when they have different tracks for a hurricane," Cuomo said. "The hurricane could hit Florida or could hit Washington or could hit New York or could miss everybody and go out to sea, right? That's sort of the forecast on the coronavirus. It could be minimal, it could affect a lot of people so prepare for the worst, hope for the best, and that's what we're doing in this state. We have mobilized for emergencies before and we're going to do it again."

What was strange about Cuomo's declaration on February 29 that COVID-19 could be like a hurricane coming in from sea—deadly or benign, depending on an unpredictable trajectory—was how little it was based in the available understanding of the virus. Just days earlier, Dr. Nancy Messonnier of the CDC had warned of significant disruptions to American life. Many countries worldwide, including China, Brazil, Italy, France, and Spain, had reported coronavirus cases. More than 50 residents of a nursing home facility in Washington state were exhibiting symptoms. Few could believe, with so much spread already taking place worldwide, coronavirus would simply "go out to sea."

A virus wasn't a hurricane, after all. Human behavior cannot impact the path of a storm. The residents of Miami or New Orleans can't quarantine themselves and force the category four hurricane to lose strength upon landfall. With a contagious virus, a government can take action to properly inform their citizens about the threat and advise behavior that can slow its spread. A government can close areas where large crowds may gather. Unlike Trump, Cuomo at least offered scenarios that were plausible, like coronavirus impacting large cities, but in his remarks, he began to display elements of Trump's wishful and ignorant thinking.

★ ★ ★

As the mythos of Cuomo the coronavirus conqueror grew, the earliest and most crucial days of his response were forgotten or ignored altogether. This is unfortunate because it was in those days—the early weeks of March in particular—when a coordinated, fact-based communication strategy akin to what was carried out in Washington State could have made a profound difference.

March 1 brought the inevitable: New York's first confirmed coronavirus case, a Manhattan woman who had recently traveled to Iran. In his 2020 memoir *American Crisis: Leadership Lessons from the COVID-19 Pandemic*, Cuomo remarks that New Yorkers are a "parochial bunch" and "our population was still fairly dismissive of the threat." Few had "reached a point of high anxiety."

"But I had," Cuomo claimed.

If this was indeed true, it was barely reflected in any of Cuomo's public statements to come. Instead of conveying his own "high anxiety" and alerting his state to the danger ahead, Cuomo insisted it was not an unusual threat at all. Reading

Cuomo's memoir, one is faced with two distinct possibilities: He was always quite anxious about COVID-19, but chose to mislead the public.

Or he had simply rewritten history.

"There is no cause for surprise—this was expected. As I said from the beginning, it was a matter of when, not if there would be a positive case of novel coronavirus in New York," Cuomo said on March 1.

Bill de Blasio, the mayor of New York City, said New Yorkers remained at "low risk" of contracting coronavirus. "As we confront this emerging outbreak, we need to separate facts from fear, and guard against stigma and panic." City officials announced that the city had received new testing kits from the CDC and that local testing could begin within a week.

Cuomo and de Blasio were fellow Democrats, though they had often been at loggerheads since de Blasio took office in 2014. When Cuomo headed the Department of Housing and Urban Development in the 1990s, de Blasio had been his subordinate, directing a regional office, and Cuomo felt a near-pathological need to remind the mayor of his junior status. Though the mayor of New York City was one of the most prestigious elected officials in America, invested with more authority than most other mayoral offices in other big cities, a governor wielded far more direct power. The State Constitution invested unique authority in the governor's office to control the outcome of the state budget each year, effectively sidelining the state legislature and local leaders.

New York City, though by far the wealthiest and most populous locality in the state, was not legally distinct, in most ways, from any other smaller suburban or rural county elsewhere. The mayor couldn't raise the city's income tax or the minimum wage without approval from Cuomo and the state legislature. If the mayor sought to toughen the city's tenant laws, Cuomo would have to sign off on the change. Even an adjustment to the speed limit on city streets or the installation of traffic cameras had to win Cuomo's approval. Education was one exception: New York City operates an independent school system under what is known as "mayoral control," but this arrangement existed at the pleasure of state legislators and Cuomo, who could revoke it whenever he'd like. The city's sprawling subway and bus system was controlled by a state agency that was under Cuomo's ultimate dominion.

Such a dynamic always created tension between mayors and governors, particularly of similar parties. Republicans Nelson Rockefeller and John Lindsay resented each other. Rudolph Giuliani was not particularly close to his Republican counterpart, George Pataki. But the Cuomo-de Blasio dynamic existed on another plane. Characterized for the seven years of their coexistence as a "feud" in the press, it was more of an obsessive, quasi-sadistic attempt to undercut de Blasio, a liberal who attempted to gain a national platform for himself in his early years as mayor.

By the time coronavirus manifested in New York, the two Democrats had been through many asymmetrical clashes, with Cuomo always holding the upper hand. At one point, a few years earlier, he had shuttered the entire subway system over a minor snowstorm while giving de Blasio 15 minutes notice. De Blasio, in a rare counterattack, would eventually accuse Cuomo of having a "vendetta" against him.

What made the coronavirus crisis different was how, initially, the two men shared a unified message to the public: you shouldn't be scared of this virus. It probably won't hurt you. Go about your life as normal.

While de Blasio, in the coming months, suffered reputational damage for downplaying COVID-19, the opposite would happen to Cuomo. Journalists, pundits, and various commentators would weave a new narrative, one of Cuomo shining between two poles of rank incompetence: Donald Trump and Bill de Blasio.

"We went through this before: Zika virus, Ebola, et cetera. But let's have some connection to the reality of the situation, and as the doctor said, catching the flu right now is a much greater risk than anything that has anything to do with coronavirus," Cuomo told reporters on February 7, less than a month before COVID-19 would start infecting and killing New Yorkers.[20]

Cuomo was not alone at this time. Few public figures were sounding the alarm in America. But Cuomo would not update his messaging dramatically in early March, when coronavirus spread unchecked through New York City. Curiously, Cuomo would talk about "fear" and "panic" being as bad or worse than the virus itself, echoing Franklin Roosevelt's address to America in 1933.

If COVID-19 isn't a hurricane going out to sea, as Cuomo likened it at the end of February, it isn't a global military conflict either, fought against enemy combatants on distant shorelines. It is quite different. For those at the epicenter, it may just be more frightening.

★ ★ ★

On March 2, Cuomo flew down from Albany to New York City, where he joined with de Blasio and the city and state health commissioners to address the first positive coronavirus case. Seated at a dais in his Midtown Manhattan office, New York's golden seal and state flag behind him, Cuomo would speak for the majority of the 34 minutes the morning press conference lasted. He sat a few feet from reporters and television cameras in the crowded room.

Cuomo, of course, was centered. The cameras would pan to him first. To his left was de Blasio, whom he had invited to the press conference, despite his dislike of the mayor. "While I was not the mayor's number one fan, a fact that was well known to the public, I made the trip to the city specifically to sit with him to show a unified front to New Yorkers," Cuomo wrote in his memoir. "An informed, consistent message was important, so by doing this event with the mayor, I could make sure we were stating the same facts."[21]

Cuomo's recollection of the press conference in his best-selling memoir skips over much of what he said, preferring to focus on efforts to provide "unbiased factual evidence" about the virus, establishing himself as a credible messenger to the public. In his memoir, Cuomo only refers to a conversation he had with his 25-year-old daughter, Mariah, in which she nervously told him "don't tell me to relax; tell me why I should be relaxed."[22]

At the Manhattan press conference, Cuomo did what public officials in Washington state had guarded against—foregrounding politicians, not public health experts. Cuomo spoke first and spoke often. De Blasio came next. Nearly 24 minutes into the press conference, well towards its conclusion, the city's health commissioner, Dr. Oxiris Barbot, finally addressed the media. Dr. Howard Zucker, New York State's health commissioner, never spoke.[23]

One theme came in strikingly clear: coronavirus wasn't so different than the ordinary flu. "So the virus will spread—yes, it will spread like, by the way, the flu spreads every year," Cuomo said.

After reiterating the facts of the first positive case in New York City and relaying his conversation with Mariah, Cuomo insisted that the "facts defeat fear." He compared COVID-19 to the Hong Kong flu in the late 1960s and the 2009 Swine flu outbreak. "Avian flu, Ebola, SARS, MERS, measles, right? So we have gone through this before." 80 percent of cases would "resolve on their own," Cuomo said. Senior citizens and those with underlying health issues were at risk—like the ordinary flu, the governor insisted—but others would be fine. He added statistics to bolster his case: "The mortality rate estimated to

INFECTION

be about 1.4 percent ... what does that mean? The normal flu mortality rate is about .6 percent and the CDC says 1.4 but they are extrapolating from what we know from countries around the world."

"The woman who has now tested positive, she's at home. She's not even in a hospital. So the perspective here is, is important. And the facts—once you know the facts, once you know the reality, it is reassuring and we should relax because that's what is dictated by the reality of the situation," Cuomo continued, insisting he understood the "anxiety" of coronavirus as a native New Yorker. "We live with anxiety but the facts don't back it up here."

That morning, Cuomo made a disastrous proclamation that would have haunted a less talented or more scrutinized politician: New York, he said, was not like China, and its healthcare system would simply repel the virus. "We're extrapolating from what happened in China, other countries. We have the best healthcare system in the world here and excuse our arrogance as New Yorkers—I speak for the mayor also on this one—we think we have the best healthcare system on the planet right here in New York."

"So when you're saying what happened in other countries versus what happened here, we don't even think it's going to be as bad as it was in other countries," Cuomo said. "We are fully coordinated, we are fully mobilized."

De Blasio echoed Cuomo, as did Barbot. The mayor boasted of New York's world-class hospital system as a primary bulwark against coronavirus. "The facts are reassuring," de Blasio said. "We don't think we have the best healthcare system in the country or the world—we know we do." (That same day, de Blasio would tweet that he was "encouraging New Yorkers to go on with their lives" and "get out on the town despite Coronavirus," offering several movie suggestions.[24])

Where were these facts coming from? COVID-19 had already spread globally and would be officially declared a pandemic only nine days later. When Cuomo was likening coronavirus to the flu, if only a tad more problematic, King County in Washington had already declared a state of emergency and was in negotiations to buy a motel where coronavirus patients could recover in isolation.[25] An infectious disease expert in Seattle estimated the virus had roughly doubled in cases every six days, and as many as 570 people could already be infected in the state.[26] At least 13 schools had already closed.

Though few observers noted it at the time, Cuomo's insistence on coronavirus bearing many similarities to the flu— "yes, it will spread like, by the way, the flu spreads every year"— would appear, in different forms, in right-wing media only days later. The argument was made repeatedly, in the early weeks of the pandemic, to protest lockdown orders handed down from city and state governments. There was no direct evidence any right-wing commentators, who likely took their cues from their own skewed information ecosystems, directly parroted Cuomo, but the similarities remained striking.

"They never quarantined anybody, H1N1 [Swine flu]. And we lost, I think ultimately it was close to, what, 13,000, 14,000, whatever thousand people. And worldwide over half a million. Isn't that correct?" asked Fox News' Sean Hannity on March 6.

"Absolutely. And over 300,000 deaths in the United States alone when all the figures were counted," replied Fox News medical contributor Marc Siegel, mistakenly recounting H1N1's global death toll as the US one. "And let me tell you something, this virus should be compared to the flu, because at worst, at worst, worst case scenario it could be the flu."[27]

In Cuomo's defense, he hadn't directly outlined a "worst case" for COVID-19. Rather, he spoke of its spread as an inevitability that would be managed because most people would not get very sick and New York's healthcare system was exceptional. It was a message, even by March 2, that was separated from the reality transpiring elsewhere.

By late February, small towns in Italy had been placed under quarantine. Wuhan was in the midst of its own severe lockdown. NYC Health + Hospitals was, indeed, the largest healthcare system in the United States, and an effective one—but Wuhan, a city of 11 million, had an enormous healthcare system of its own, with 6.51 hospital beds per 1,000 people[28], compared to the mere 2.47 beds per 1,000 people available in the New York metro area.

Cuomo and de Blasio had few facts to base their confidence on. Their blithe approach would prove deadly. In the months to come, Cuomo, like many liberal commentators, would blame the federal government for not alerting them to COVID-19's threat sooner.

"In the last week of January an adviser to the president, Peter Navarro, sent an internal memo that should have set off alarm bells. It said that the coronavirus was not contained to China and could possibly affect 200 million Americans," Cuomo wrote in his memoir. "The memo went on to say the virus could result in one to two million lives lost—more casualties than have been sustained in any war the nation has ever been engaged in … Who read the memo? What was done as a result of this memo? Absolutely nothing."[29]

Cuomo is right: had the memo been made public and Trump taken it seriously, many lives would have been saved. But the governors, mayors, and county executives of Washington and California, where COVID-19 was also spreading unchecked, didn't have access to this information either. They were not likening the virus to a hurricane that could fizzle at sea or to past outbreaks that didn't traumatize the American populace. They were allowing public health officials to communicate the threat plainly to the public.

New York would lag behind Washington and California by days—and with coronavirus spreading so rapidly, the delays and muddled messaging cost thousands of lives.

★ ★ ★

On March 3, New York had its second positive case, this time in the city of New Rochelle, just north of New York City. Over the next week, coronavirus would spread rapidly in the area, and Cuomo would announce a one-mile "containment" zone in the city, closing schools, houses of worship, and other large facilities.[30] Such a policy, if well-intentioned, would create the mistaken impression that coronavirus was not already spreading and infecting residents in New York City, who were still going to bars, restaurants, and living life normally. The National Guard, meanwhile, deployed to New Rochelle.

The press briefings were daily now. Though cases were growing—there were 22 new coronavirus cases and five hospitalizations by March 6—Cuomo's tenor had not shifted notably. As public health officials urged frequent hand-washing and mouth-covering when coughing or sneezing, Cuomo was still focused on calming nerves, explaining COVID-19 in the context of flu season.

"Should we shake hands? I have doctors who say to me every flu season, you should say, people should not shake hands," Cuomo said at the March 6 briefing. "They say that to me every flu season. I've never said that. Why? Because I'm a politician, I shake hands. You shouldn't hug. They've said that during a normal flu season. I've never said that either. I'm of Italian-American descent, I'm a hugger."

"But precautions during the flu season, don't shake hands and don't hug," he continued. "During this season with coronavirus, yeah if you want to take precautions, don't shake hands, don't hug. Tell the other person so you don't offend them."

The elderly and the immuno-compromised should guard against coronavirus, Cuomo said, but that was true of the flu too. No need to panic. No need to indulge in what he called the "daily mania" of fretting over rising cases.

"I'm worried about undue fear and anxiety, hence why I'm constantly trying to communicate facts," Cuomo said that day. "I have friends who are HIV-positive, who are battling cancer, who have compromised immune systems, they have to be careful and they have to be more careful than usual. But, that is what this is, which is the same as it would be for the normal flu. Right? Who does the flu normally affect? Seniors, immune compromised, people with underlying illnesses."

Cuomo went on to belabor a point that would soon join the rhetorical arsenal of right-wing politicians who dismissed the grave threat coronavirus posed: more testing would produce higher positive cases, and that meant there was little to worry about.

"I'm perturbed that people get anxious every time the number goes up. The number has to go up if you continue to test. The number can't go down right. We're not going to detect fewer cases than yesterday. The number has to go up—that's why we're testing," he said. (Months later, the Republican governors of Florida and Texas would mistakenly attribute their own spikes in coronavirus cases to increased testing. "As you test more, you will see more cases," Ron DeSantis, the governor of Florida and a close Trump ally, said in June. "As we've gotten into May, and then really June, it's been consistently in about the 30,000 test results a day."[31])

What was actually happening in New York City? As many as 10,700 people could have been infected with coronavirus by the beginning of March, a Northeastern University study would later find.[32] And New York wasn't alone. San Francisco had as many as 9,700 cases, a far higher percentage of their populace. Seattle was coursing with 2,300.

Each day that passed without some kind of restriction on movement and crowding meant more cases and eventually mass death. Neither Cuomo nor de Blasio could have guessed the number of cases was so high, but public health experts were already extraordinarily concerned about the potential for large outbreaks in big cities. "We may be entering a period of accelerating cases. The country could look very different over [the] next two weeks," tweeted Scott Gottlieb, Trump's former Food and Drug Administration commissioner, on March 7. "This is a dangerous virus. We have faced worse, and prevailed. People will suffer and die."[33]

The same day as Gottlieb's tweet, Cuomo declared a state of emergency, expediting procurement of cleaning and testing supplies, as well as the leasing of lab spaces. But a more significant move had been made days earlier, when Cuomo won new and extraordinarily expansive emergency powers, attaching them to a legislative push for $40 million in funding to combat COVID-19. Few legislators, as the bill was hurried through in the dead of night, understood exactly what Cuomo had sought.

"I'm scared or concerned because I don't know what the governor has in mind," said State Assemblyman Richard Gottfried, the longest-tenured lawmaker and the chairman of the Health Committee.[34]

Lawmakers had learned on the afternoon of March 2 that legislation would be coming to the floor from the governor's office. The state's health commissioner, Howard Zucker, met with Assembly Democrats for a briefing, making no mention of the need for additional emergency power.

The state legislature hardly debated the bill, passing it after midnight. Though New York law already allowed Cuomo to suspend provisions of any state or local statute that would delay in coping with a declared disaster, the new measure went further, broadening the definition of disaster from a "past occurrence" to something that was "impending." The new law added "disease outbreak" to a list of triggering events alongside "epidemic," and handed Cuomo new power to issue directives "necessary to cope with" a broad list of potential disasters, from tornados to cyberattacks to volcanic eruptions.

The definition of disasters was general enough to worry civil libertarians that Cuomo, a governor who already enjoyed aggressively wielding executive power, could abuse the new law in a wide array of circumstances. Part of the challenge of understanding the expansion was the lack of specificity in the bill language. Adding sweeping emergency powers could theoretically justify all kinds of maneuvers, like the declaration of martial law, unilateral travel restrictions, and mass quarantines. The New

York Civil Liberties Union compared the law, unfavorably, to anti-terrorism provisions passed after 9/11 that were never used to prosecute terrorism.

The limits of the new language were largely unknown.

"One of my mentors was born inside an internment camp," said Yuh-Line Niou, an Asian-American state lawmaker, referring to the unlawful detention of Japanese-American citizens during World War II. "I have an innate fear of what would happen if we allow our government to be able to weaponize fear and to be able to make a directive and have the power to order private citizens to do something without any checks and balances."

FEAR

Ironically, the coming coronavirus crisis would showcase Cuomo's relative weakness and indecision, rather than a mere authoritarian instinct. Like Trump, who was derided as a fascist for four years and then failed dramatically to wield power against the virus, Cuomo's performance would belie, perhaps, a more troubling reality: New York State was running out of time.

By March 8, there were 105 confirmed cases statewide. New York City now had 12. As panic began to slowly spread in the city, with more looking warily to China and Europe as a preview of what was to come, Cuomo refused to back off his central contention: fear was worse than coronavirus itself.

Leaping into his state-issued helicopter, Cuomo had arrived at the suburban village of New Hyde Park, just beyond the border of New York City. He held his press briefing at Northwell Health, where he aimed to get FDA approval to run more coronavirus tests. (Northwell Health got that approval.) Rather than sit in Albany's Red Room or his Midtown office, Cuomo stood behind a podium with his health commissioner, Howard Zucker. Behind them, physicians in white lab coats stoically looked on.

It was a Sunday. Cuomo donned his dark dress coat and tan slacks, no tie at his neck. Zucker wore a similar ensemble.

"There is a level of fear here that is not connected to the facts. There is more fear, more anxiety, than the facts would justify," Cuomo declared. "Okay, that is why I want to make sure everyone understands what we are dealing with. You look at the facts here."[35]

What did the facts say, in Cuomo's estimation? COVID-19 wasn't unusual at all. "This is not the Ebola virus, this is not the SARS virus, this is a virus that we have a lot of information on. Johns Hopkins has been tracking this coronavirus— almost every case. Johns Hopkins has been tracking the 100,000 cases. What happens? For most people, you get the virus, you get sick, you stay home. Most people have mild symptoms, most people don't get hospitalized."

Four days earlier, officials in Washington state had urged, unambiguously, all employers who could do so to allow their employees to work from home. Microsoft, in coordination with county and state officials, led the way. Cuomo's advice was milder, buried deeper in his briefing: "To the extent the private sector company can say, 'Stay at home, nonessential workers. Work from home.' More and more this is a digital economy. To the extent workers can work at home, let them work at home. We want to reduce the density."

Invoking Ebola and SARS, two viruses that devastated countries elsewhere but had little impact on the United States, was guaranteed to lull and reassure New Yorkers. SARS had been a curiosity limited to Asia. Ebola brought a brief panic six years earlier, but only a lone medical doctor had become infected in New York. When he was treated, Bill de Blasio embraced him in a hug, to much applause.[36] Within a few months, the fear had subsided, and there had been no disruption of everyday life. Broadway shows went on. Museums remained packed. Restaurants, bars, and comedy clubs teemed with patrons. Times Square, as always, hummed with tourists.

Each day, new Ebola and SARS cases didn't rapidly increase in New York. For anyone who paid attention to the news, coronavirus was clearly going to be different. By March 10, there were 173 confirmed cases statewide and 17 in New York City. A day later, the statewide total was 216.[37] Across the country, Seattle had announced the closure of its public schools, finalizing a weeks-long process that acclimated residents to a new, distressing normal: life curtailed, life indoors.

March 11 would be remembered as a pivot point in history for coronavirus in America. The virus had been a backdrop for weeks, hovering in newspapers, tormenting the stock market, and feeding anxiety among those who understood epidemiology. It was a slowly building roar, threatening to break open the normalcy Americans still clung to. Right before tipoff, a basketball player for the Utah Jazz tested positive for the virus. The game was postponed. Shortly after, the NBA announced it was suspending its season.

That night, Donald Trump addressed the nation from the Oval Office for just the second time since taking office. All these years later, the sight of the former reality TV star could still seem surreal, particularly for native New Yorkers who recalled Trump as little more than cultural kitsch for much of their adult lives. Sniffling while haltingly reading off a teleprompter, Trump folded his hand on his desk and approximated, to the best of his limited ability, the intonations and gestures of the American presidents he had watched on television.

Speaking for 10 minutes, Trump announced that most travel from Europe, following China, would be suspended for the next 30 days. He also said financial relief measures would be imminent. "No nation is more prepared or more resilient than the United States," Trump said. "We have the best economy, the most advanced healthcare, and the most talented doctors, scientists, and researchers anywhere in the world."

Cuomo and de Blasio had made similar proclamations about New York City just nine days prior. Exceptionalism, for New York and America, would beat the virus. Hours before Trump spoke, Cuomo had been in Albany. His tone had begun to shift subtly. The public university systems of New York City and New York State would end in-person instruction the following week, he said. Though he had not confirmed whether the annual St. Patrick's Day Parade, the largest such celebration in the world, would be canceled, a decision came late Wednesday that a postponement had come for the first time in more than 250 years.[38] Celebrations in Chicago and Boston had already been canceled.

De Blasio was waffling too. As recently as March 9, he had wanted the parade to go on, and generally urged New Yorkers to continue eating out, shopping, and enjoying their city. Outside of the public eye, de Blasio was clashing with his Health Department, which was pleading with him to enact restrictions and warn residents about the severity of coronavirus. In early March, de Blasio had blocked an effort at "sentinel surveillance," which would have asked local hospitals to provide the New York City Department of Health with swabs collected from people who had flu-like symptoms and had tested negative for influenza. De Blasio's office, one Health Department official said, wanted to stem mass panic, since sentinel surveillance would have probably revealed what they mostly suspected: hundreds, if not thousands, of people were already infected with the virus.[39]

Cuomo, like de Blasio, was not willing to concede that COVID-19 posed a catastrophic threat to New York. This became apparent in his remarks at the end of his March 11 briefing, when he again compared coronavirus—a rapidly spreading contagion with no known cure—to the ordinary flu. First, Cuomo said Ebola was much more frightening. "I understand it's a virus, I understand it sounds like a bad science fiction movie. This is not the Ebola virus, we've dealt with that. That was a much more dangerous, frightening virus."

"The facts here," Cuomo continued, "actually reduce the anxiety."

How?

One, Cuomo said, most coronavirus patients in New York were at home, not hospitalized. They were recovering.

"Let's go back to China, to the first case, and track all of the cases and find out what happened," the governor continued, ticking off his favored facts. "121,000 cases from the beginning, 4,000 deaths. 66,000 people recovered, 50,000 pending cases. 4,000 deaths are terrible, yes, no doubt."

"How many people died in the United States from the flu last year? Roughly 80,000 from the flu. So, again, perspective."

Perspective, Cuomo urged. The flu had never led to a travel ban or a canceled NBA season. It had never reordered society. There was, indeed, perspective to be gained from the coronavirus, watching it tear through large parts of the world before landing in the United States, but this was not what Cuomo was calling for. Coronavirus appeared, even by then, to be twice as contagious as the flu and require far longer hospital stays. It was much deadlier. There was no vaccine.

As public health officials began to recommend lockdowns, invoking the flu was the most convenient, ignorant rebuttal. Hadn't we maintained a strong, open economy with tens of thousands of flu deaths annually? Trump and Cuomo, for a brief moment, were almost in agreement.

"So last year 37,000 Americans died from the common Flu. It averages between 27,000 and 70,000 per year," Trump tweeted on March 9. "Nothing is shut down, life & the economy go on. At this moment there are 546 confirmed cases of CoronaVirus, with 22 deaths. Think about that!"

Cuomo's memoir dwells little on March 11, the day American life was wrenched in a horrific new direction. He claims, falsely, "many people thought I was overreacting" when he announced the transition to remote learning for the city and state university systems. No public official openly criticized the move. He mulls over the anti-Asian sentiment Trump had stirred up about "the China virus" but does not refer, in any way, to the comments he made at his press briefing. "The communication strategy was everything," he writes.

The next day brought changes from both Cuomo and de Blasio. In a bow to the severity of the virus, Cuomo banned gatherings larger than 500 people, shutting down Madison Square Garden and Broadway. Public schools across the city and state were exempted. De Blasio, in his own public remarks, appeared humbled, his voice seeming to quiver with the anxiety that much of the city was now feeling. He had, at last, declared a state of emergency for New York City.

"We have to fully understand that this is the shape of things to come," the mayor said. "It feels like the world turned upside down in just the course of a few hours."[40]

Coronavirus was plainly spreading everywhere. There were 95 confirmed cases in the city, up 42 from the previous day. For the first time, de Blasio acknowledged the cold, terrifying reality of the virus: he expected the city could have 1,000 cases by next week, with 20 percent requiring hospitalization.

"We're getting into a situation where the only analogy is war," he said.

The major shutdown orders of the previous 24 hours had come from Cuomo's office, including the cancellation of the St. Patrick's Day Parade, which wended through the streets de Blasio governed. In almost all instances, the state government enjoyed legal dominion over city government, and could override any local law or action taken. De Blasio was the mayor of New York City, but Cuomo now operated as a mayor *and* governor—no move, consequential or not, could proceed without his approval.

In ordinary times, Cuomo could cede some control to de Blasio, acknowledging the important role he played in the governing of more than eight million people. But in wartime, with his own vast emergency powers, there was no need to treat de Blasio as anything more than a nettlesome subordinate.

If Cuomo were acting, as he insisted, on the basis of science and fact alone, this would not have been such a poor development for the people of New York City. De Blasio was a known micromanager and equivocator, frustrating his staff with his singular blend of self-righteousness and indecision. He was not a crisis manager, and would never be one.

The problem was Cuomo wasn't one either.

Coronavirus isn't so different than the flu, he had said. It isn't as threatening as Ebola. The fear is worse than the reality. Cases were rising, he insisted, simply because New York State, thanks to his aggressive maneuvering, was testing a lot more people. Unwittingly parroting—or inspiring—Republican talking points, Cuomo was inventing a version of reality that did not square with imminent suffering and death.

On March 12, Cuomo spoke about the shutdown orders, the state's push to immediately increase testing, and the ability of hospitals to increase their surge capacity, adding excess beds. The mandates handed down were much more urgent. Yet Cuomo, once more, couched his remarks, attempting to *decrease* concern about coronavirus.

"I know the hysteria is high. I know the political environment superheats everything," Cuomo said. He once more referred to Johns Hopkins University's tracking of coronavirus. "127,000, 4,000 fatalities. 68,000 of the 127,000 have recovered and 54,000 are pending. Those are the facts. Those are the numbers. Well, this one thinks this, this one opinion, yeah, opinion, opinion, opinion. These are the facts and these are the numbers."[41]

What about the flu?

"It is worse than the flu in terms of the numbers, yes," Cuomo acknowledged. "We don't want to lose anyone, that's unfortunate. But it's more being able to handle this situation governmentally, operationally. Being able to make it all work, and that's what we're planning on right now."

In New York City, local elected officials were demanding the city shutter the public schools, following the lead of San Francisco and Seattle. On Friday, March 13, Corey Johnson, the speaker of the City Council, demanded de Blasio close the schools. Inside the mayor's office, there was understandable consternation—school closures would convey to the public that coronavirus was a threat like no other, but a system serving one million kids was also a lifeline to low-income families, who relied on it for free breakfast and lunch. Working-class parents couldn't easily arrange babysitters. Remote-learning was untested. Still, with coronavirus ravaging the city already, reducing crowding everywhere possible had to be the ultimate priority.

Cuomo, in this instance, allowed de Blasio to make the final decision, because it was the most politically difficult. It was a favored tactic of Cuomo's office, one that could be executed with such an inept opponent: take credit for the easy wins and let de Blasio absorb blame for all the failure, even when the state government held all the real power and influence.

Three years earlier, the state-controlled subway had been deteriorating, with increased delays and rotting infrastructure dating back to the 1930s. Cuomo insisted he had no real control of the subways, even though the Metropolitan Transportation Authority was a state agency, with Cuomo appointing the chair and a plurality of board members. It had been a particularly absurd claim to make in light of the fact that Cuomo had rung in the new year staging a lavish ribbon cutting for the Second Avenue Subway on the Upper East Side, taking full credit for the achievement. Cuomo's new interpretation of the subway system, seemingly invented wholesale in 2017, mystified transit experts and veterans of state government. "The governor of New York controls the MTA," said Tom Doherty, who was deputy secretary to one of Cuomo's predecessors, George Pataki.[42]

Cuomo controlled the public schools of New York State until he didn't. Then, it was up to the localities. Though he would gain a reputation in subsequent weeks for tough-talk and foresight, Cuomo's decision to order a statewide shutdown of schools lagged behind what governors had done in many other major states. Before Cuomo forced de Blasio's hand to close the city's schools on the evening of March 15, the states of Michigan, Wisconsin, Ohio, Florida, and Illinois had already issued statewide orders for closures.[43] The day before, Cuomo was still leaving the decisions up to individual school districts, since these were the most wrenching calls to make. Monroe County, which includes the city of Rochester, had announced the closure of their public schools on March 14.[44]

March 13 was a Friday. March 15, a Sunday. This meant one final weekend for residents of New York City to pack restaurants, nightclubs, and bars, thronging city streets like any ordinary time. By not ordering their closure, Cuomo and de Blasio undoubtedly created more opportunities for the virus to spread—by Monday, there were 463 confirmed cases, an enormous leap from 95 just days ago.[45] At least here, neither man was far *behind* the two other cities most impacted, Seattle and San Francisco. Jay Inslee, the Washington governor, ordered a statewide shutdown of bars and restaurants on March 15. California Governor Gavin Newsom advised that same day for bars, wineries, and brew pubs—though not restaurants—to close.[46]

The weekend was de Blasio's bid for infamy. Cuomo's longstanding, wildly misleading comparisons of coronavirus to the flu never garnered much media attention, but de Blasio's unrelated statements did. Much of this could be blamed on de Blasio himself, for his perplexing words and deeds. Some blame, too, lay in the nature of the New York media market, which typically reserved far more scrutiny for the mayor than the governor. All week, de Blasio had foolishly advised New Yorkers to enjoy the city as they always had, the way prior leaders may have urged on a skittish populace after a terrorist attack. "If you love your neighborhood bar, go there now," de Blasio said as late March 15.[47]

New Yorkers largely took de Blasio's advice. On Friday, Cuomo had mandated venues reduce capacity by 50 percent, but without any kind of shutdown order, enforcement hardly existed. Pianos, the Lower East Side mainstay, was just one bar that was jammed with customers—perhaps even more than usual. "Hundo! Hundo. We're 100 percent concerned. Definitely," said a woman milling outside the venue. When asked why she was going in the bar with her friends anyway, she blamed her own intoxication—and local guidance. "Because I'm drunk! It's my friend's 25th birthday. I'm waiting for the government to tell me I should be more concerned, if I'm being honest."[48]

Some restaurants, out of caution, had begun to shutter. Without an executive order from either Cuomo or de Blasio, though, the vast majority of establishments would operate as much as they could, taking in cash before being told to close.

The weekend gone, de Blasio drew further scorn when he worked out at his gym in the Brooklyn neighborhood of Park Slope, an 11-mile drive from the mayor's residence at Gracie Mansion. De Blasio's Monday morning visit to the Park Slope

YMCA came just hours before Cuomo's mandate that all gyms statewide close.

At any moment that weekend, regarding either schools or nightlife closures, Cuomo could have overrode de Blasio. He chose not to. He would get one more crucial opportunity to do so, and this time he took it—but this time it was the bumbling mayor who had more foresight.

On March 15, Cuomo briefed reporters in Albany. Accompanied by his PowerPoint slides, a staple of his presentations for a decade, he was clearly gaining an audience as petrified New Yorkers were turning to him for leadership and guidance. He noted the new, spaced seating for journalists arrayed in the ornate Red Room, a concession to social distancing guidelines. The "wave," he said, could "break" on the hospital system and "overwhelm it."

Cuomo, a deft tactician, was already positioning himself to deflect any blame he could take for New York's tragically delayed response—both in words and in actions—to COVID-19. "Listen to the cable news all day, 'well, why didn't we start testing earlier, why weren't we more prepared?' That's all about yesterday, right? That's all recriminations, that's blame, we should've done this, we should've done that, we should've done this," Cuomo railed. "I'm governor—I am here today, I'm focused on what I need today to prepare for tomorrow. And that's what everybody should focus on."

"You want to do a retrospective on who should've done what when and who's to blame, put a pin in it and do it afterwards.

Let's be constructive, which is focusing on today and tomorrow," he continued. "There's an old military expression that management officials use: 'don't fight the last war.' This is not about what happened yesterday. We are looking at a new war that no one has seen before."

At last, when it was far too late, Cuomo bowed to the reality that coronavirus was not Ebola, SARS, not the ordinary flu. It was something, obviously, far more contagious and widespread. "This is a case of first impression for this nation. We have never fought a virus like this with this potential consequence."

It was a striking break from just four days earlier, when Cuomo told New Yorkers to put coronavirus in proper "perspective," since around 80,000 people per year died from the flu. The governor was done with flu-talk. The next day, after de Blasio had been ridiculed for rushing to the Park Slope Y, both men would speak on coronavirus with a new gravity.

But it was too late. On March 16, de Blasio said he was doing his best to allow city employees to work from home, though Seattle had been encouraging this for nearly two weeks. The mayor promised to build out thousands of hospital beds to meet the coming surge. Schools, bars, restaurants, and nightclubs were shutting down. The city, on the eve of St. Patrick's Day, was changing inalterably, verging on a kind of mass shutdown never seen in its history. In Washington, the CDC recommended people avoid gathering in groups of more than 10 people.

Across the country, local governments in California, with Newsom's blessing, dramatically escalated tactics: six Bay Area counties, in coordination with one another, issued shelter-in-place orders on March 16, to take effect the next day. Only businesses deemed essential could operate physically. Everyone was directed to stay inside their homes as much as possible for at least the next three weeks. At the time, it was the strictest measure of its kind in the continental United States.[49]

"We were seeing a tipping point here in Santa Clara County with exponential growth of our cases," said Dr. Sara Cody, health officer for the county, at a news conference that Monday. "Over the weekend, I had a discussion with fellow health officers in the Bay Area and we realized that we are one region, and that what's happening in Santa Clara County today will soon be happening in the adjacent jurisdictions. We decided collectively we need to take swift action as soon as possible to prevent further spread."

The order came as 472 tested positive for COVID-19—statewide. In New York City alone, as of Monday, there were 463 positive cases. The next day, that number would balloon to 814.[50] The virus was out of control, racing through apartment buildings, hospitals, and nursing homes, sickening many thousands. Each day that passed represented another opportunity lost to keep people healthy and alive.

There was no satisfying historical parallel for the terror New Yorkers were now experiencing. Though fear of another attack would linger for years, September 11 was confined to a single cataclysmic day, and the city would regain its rhythm as clubs,

bars, museums, movie theaters, and baseball stadiums enthusiastically opened their doors, New Yorkers urged to do their duty
and live as they always had. To celebrate—to have a drink with
friends, play basketball in the park, or take in a concert—was to
make a stand against fear, and know the city's civic leaders were
cheering you on each day.

Coronavirus demanded something entirely different.

The next day, March 17, de Blasio appeared to understand
what was happening to his city. He was term-limited, due to
leave at the end of next year, and he had spent much of 2019 mus-
ing about and then running for president, failing to garner any
support, and dropping out before the Iowa caucuses. His national
ambitions were widely lampooned. Among the agenda-setting
journalists of the city, he was never taken seriously, viewed as a
gawky, feckless liberal too consumed with his national standing
and disinterested in the machinery of government. He thirsted
for a following he never earned. He didn't seem, to the reporters
who covered him daily, to particularly *enjoy* the job of mayor,
which invited daily agita a pugnacious politician—a Michael
Bloomberg, a Rudy Giuliani—was demanded to rise above, or
at least meet head-on. After 9/11, a once unpopular Giuliani was
deemed America's mayor, lionized for trying to console the city
in his final months in office. There would be no similar valedictions for de Blasio.

Speaking from City Hall, de Blasio had a new, stark warning
for the city he still led. "All New Yorkers, even though a decision has not been made by the city or the state, I think that all

New Yorkers should be prepared right now for the possibility of a shelter-in-place order." The mayor noted that he was looking to California and Italy, in the midst of its own severe outbreak, for guidance. "It has not happened yet but it is definitely a possibility at this point. I believe that decision should be made in the next 48 hours, and it's a very, a very difficult decision."

The mayor said he had a "variety of conversations" with Cuomo's office. "We respect the role of the state always," de Blasio said. "I just think it's decision time."

It was the first time de Blasio had called for a drastic new restriction *ahead* of Cuomo. Until then, the two men had been in relative sync, echoing one another in their belief that New York, with its own exceptional healthcare infrastructure and gusto, could will the virus away. Cuomo, possessed of better instincts, had never made de Blasio's obvious errors—rushing to a gym, goading people to keep drinking at their favorite bars—but he had spent much of the month griping about the "hysteria" surrounding coronavirus. It was no accident, in most Seattle and San Francisco news stories and television segments, that public health officials were those often quoted, allowed to speak frankly about the danger of the virus. Politicians opined too, but in concert with their physicians and epidemiologists—and not always first.

In New York, it had become the Cuomo show. And the governor clearly liked it. "My briefings were garnering tremendous attention," he boasts in his memoir. "They were broadcast live on national networks for up to two hours per day. We had tens of millions of viewers."[51] Cuomo believed that this newfound fame could be used to get the attention of Trump, a compulsive cable television watcher. "Donald Trump did not have the only microphone. I had one too. And I had something else: credibility."

There was little disagreement among public health experts that by mid-March, New York City desperately needed a shelter-in-place order. Residents needed to stay indoors as much as possible to reduce the spread of the virus. Only social distancing could slow down transmission enough to preserve hospital capacity, now gravely threatened. De Blasio, on March 17, was merely echoing a consensus, looking elsewhere and watching how leaders, reacting to a darkening future, were making decisions. If San Francisco, with far fewer confirmed cases, was willing to shut itself down indefinitely, then New York City had to do the same.

Cuomo did not agree. He reminded reporters, throughout that Tuesday, that de Blasio had no authority to take such an action—and shouldn't anyway. In a crisis, the reality of governing was laid bare, and the mayor of New York City had the statutory authority to do virtually nothing without Cuomo's explicit permission. Shelter-in-place was up to him. It would be his order to make.

And he wasn't going to make it.

"We hear 'New York City is going to quarantine itself.' That is not true. That cannot happen. It cannot happen legally," Cuomo declared not long after de Blasio's announcement. "No city in the state can quarantine itself without state approval. And

I have no interest whatsoever and no plan whatsoever to quarantine any city."

In addition to speaking daily with reporters, the governor was making regular one-on-one appearances on cable news networks, and connected Tuesday evening with CNN's Jake Tapper. Instead of embracing de Blasio's call—or at least conceding it was a possibility—Cuomo dismissed it entirely.

"My job is to make sure that the state has a coordinated plan and it works everywhere. I don't think shelter-in-place really works for one locality," Cuomo said on CNN. "I'm a New York City boy, born and raised if you can't tell, and we're very good at getting around the rules. You say shelter-in-place if you stay in New York City, I'll go stay with my sister in Westchester, right? I'll go stay with a buddy in the neighboring suburb of Nassau," he continued. "So I don't think you can really do a policy like that just in one part of the state. So I don't think it works."

"As a matter of fact, I'm going so far that I don't even think you can do a statewide policy."[52]

Strangely, for such an eventful day—perhaps the most pivotal of all in the first three weeks of coronavirus in New York—Cuomo hardly reflects on it in his memoir. He makes no mention of de Blasio's declaration in the chapter reserved for March 17. The chapter itself is brief, less than three pages, and mostly recounts a phone call with Trump, who expressed frustration about an interview Cuomo held with his younger brother Chris, a well-known CNN host. "I don't understand why you're trying to work with him," Cuomo recounts his top aide, Melissa

DeRosa, telling him shortly after the phone call. "It's like Lucy with the football. It's impossible; *he's* impossible."[53]

In such a self-aggrandizing project, there is a perverse logic to what Cuomo includes and what he omits. Nowhere, in his recollections of early March, are transcriptions of his most perplexing remarks—the repeated comparisons to the flu, the insistence that the fear of the virus was worse than the virus itself. De Blasio, predictably, does not make many appearances. Cuomo does not tell us how he reacted to de Blasio's call for a shelter-in-place order or what his top aides, let alone his health commissioner, thought about such an idea.

What was exceedingly clear to most public health officials, inside and outside state government, was that New York City was running out of time. It was now a matter of mitigating death, taking whatever steps necessary to keep people indoors and away from each other. Ordering New Yorkers inside was the final, obvious step, inarguable to anyone with an even rudimentary understanding of epidemiology.

Cuomo's public comments on March 17, on a closer inspection, made little sense. Why couldn't a city of eight million people have its own shelter-in-place order? Some people had relatives in the suburbs, but many did not. The wealthiest had fled anyway, as an analysis of cellphone location data would later reveal. If regional coordination was the issue, why couldn't Cuomo, the most powerful man in the state, initiate such coordination immediately? The county executives of Nassau, Suffolk, and Westchester counties were all Democrats and close allies of the governor's office. In California, *six* different counties had already coordinated on a shelter-in-place order. Cuomo, in possession of far more clout in his own state than Newsom in California, could have placed a few phone calls and launched the process that night.

He didn't. No obvious rationale was offered. On March 18, New York City had 1,871 confirmed cases, far exceeding the 1,000 de Blasio had predicted a week earlier. Eleven people were dead. Since testing was hard to come by within the city, it was estimated many thousands more had contracted coronavirus, and soon the city would start tabulating suspected cases. Cuomo had not budged from his declaration: no shelter-in-place for New York City. "I talked to the governor about that model. We're having a good conversation, a productive conversation," de Blasio said in a radio interview that day, explaining why he hadn't yet won the governor's support.[54]

That same day, Cuomo issued another executive order, cementing his authority over New York City and every other county in the state. The decree was sweeping: no locality could issue any emergency order or executive order pertaining to COVID-19 without the approval of the State Department of Health.[55] This ended, in essence, any vestiges of local control left in New York. De Blasio, the mayor of New York City, could not take *any* action on coronavirus without the approval of the state. The executive order guaranteed, by law, de Blasio could not lock down his city, even if he wanted to.

Cuomo, indeed, was a man of action. It was only that the action he was taking generated *inaction*. No one would upstage him now.

As California and Washington took unprecedented steps to slow the spread of the virus, Cuomo continued on making egregiously inaccurate public comments about COVID-19, breeding unwarranted complacency and possibly, for a time, echoing and inspiring Fox News rhetoric. Why wasn't Cuomo facing more pressure to act?

An alternate reality was unfolding, one that would favor Cuomo mightily. The governor was not merely a politician on par with those who had taken similar or more prescient actions, including Jay Inslee, Dow Constantine, Gavin Newsom, or London Breed, the mayor of San Francisco. He was *above* them all in the most rarefied air of American politics. He was ascending, swiftly, from parochial power broker to national hero.

New York's news media was entirely on his side.

On March 16, Ben Smith, the *New York Times'* new and influential media columnist, published a column with an unforgettable headline: "Andrew Cuomo is the Control Freak We Need Right Now." Smith, a longtime reporter and editor who had worked at multiple New York newspapers, argued that Cuomo was the perfect fit for the current crisis:

> He has passed marriage equality, cut deals with Republicans, meddled incessantly in the running of the subway system. The people most passionate about

politics these days—the New Left and the Trump-led right—dislike him because he governs as both a social liberal and a friend of business. Many moderate and liberal politicians, who ought in theory to like Mr. Cuomo, simply fear him.

And yet Mr. Cuomo has emerged as the executive best suited for the coronavirus crisis, as President Trump flails and New York City Mayor Bill de Blasio wrestles haltingly with a crucial decision and then heads to the gym.

The governor has been the clearest and most decisive of the three, relentless behind the scenes and open about the risks. He has publicly worried over his daughters and his 88-year-old mother, and put state prisoners to work making hand sanitizer. He's alternated between sweetness and confrontation with Mr. Trump, as he would with a wayward upstate legislator.

Even many of his critics say the very qualities that make him abrasive in ordinary interactions are serving him well now.[56]

Smith's argument—resting, in part, on a style and aesthetic of governance—would become the dominant narrative in the coming months. It was both top-down and bottom-up driven, a product of elite media and a genuine attachment New Yorkers felt to Cuomo in these dire times, so otherwise bereft of stable leadership. Trump, of course, had long abdicated that role. And de Blasio's last-minute flight to the gym had cemented his reputation as a self-involved, oblivious politician. Cuomo, hectoring and commanding and occasionally vulnerable—indeed, he was prone to digressions on his daughters and his elderly mother—could easily slip in and fill the void.

Curiously, Smith and others made relatively few arguments about policy specifics related to Cuomo's response, and entirely ignored the many times he dismissed the threat of the pandemic in March. "He holds news conferences filled with facts and (accurate) numbers almost every day. He explains systems and challenges and decision-making with a command that Mr. Trump lacks. He even models social distancing by having speakers stay six feet apart from one another," Smith wrote.

If the numbers were accurate—the flu deaths, those who were sick and recovering from COVID-19—they had been placed into a catastrophically misleading context, convincing New Yorkers coronavirus would be like Ebola and SARS, viruses that hardly impacted the city at all. Modeling social distancing was a low bar to clear, particularly when he had already mused about his politician's love of a good handshake during flu season.

"But the governor's great strength has always been his capacity to bend the bureaucracy to his will, and he has done that in recent days: pushing to get tests running in state labs, nudging the mayor to shut schools, coordinating a tristate shutdown of most commerce," Smith argued.

Cuomo had ramped up testing, creating several drive-in sites and haranguing Trump for expedited FDA approval. This mattered. But Cuomo had also misled the public into believing rising caseloads would simply be tied to testing capacity. He had mirrored right-wing arguments. "Nudging" the mayor was also a peculiar characterization for the most powerful politician in the state, someone who could decide on his own to shut schools, as governors had already done before him in other states. If Cuomo were in such command, schools everywhere might have announced closures days earlier. Yet the next day, after Smith's column appeared, a member of the *New York Times* editorial board declared "this may prove to be the finest moment of Andrew Cuomo's public life."[57]

There was something else about Cuomo too—he was alluring, entrancing. "I need Cuomo's measured bullying, his love of circumventing the federal government, his sparring with increasingly incompetent city leadership," wrote Rebecca Fishbein on the website Jezebel, in a piece entitled "Help, I think I'm in love with Andrew Cuomo???" "Not only that, but the less contact I have with other humans, the more I start to think of Cuomo as my only friend."

"I swooned when he told a reporter he had his own workout routine. I have watched a clip of him and brother Chris Cuomo bickering about their mother at least 20 times. I think I have a crush???" (Later that afternoon, Cuomo would call Fishbein herself, claiming to have read her story.)[58]

A few days later, on March 22, *Vogue*'s Molly Jong-Fast admitted that she never much cared for Cuomo before, but the pandemic had changed her view entirely. "All of a sudden, I love Governor Cuomo, his soothing Queens accent, his stories about his dad Mario (himself a three-term governor of New York) and his 88-year-old mother Matilda." In the piece, which carried the headline "Why We Are Crushing on Andrew Cuomo Right Now," Jong-Fast wrote that she felt a "pang of jealously" after reading that Fishbein got to have her own phone call with the governor. "He was MY competent governor/imaginary boyfriend. Rebecca can have the horrible, self-congratulatory mayor (and failed presidential candidate) who is always screaming at me through the TV."

Contrasting Cuomo with Trump and de Blasio—as Smith and other pundits had done—Jong-Fast said his press briefings, now routinely occurring in the late morning, were a lasting comfort. "As the pandemic rages, and my city is decimated and I watch the empty streets from my window, I'm comforted by Andrew Cuomo's 11:00 a.m. press conferences, which both the local news and national networks are showing," she wrote. "It's nice to know that someone is governing, that someone is keeping track of the hospital beds and the ventilators and the masks, and keeping the pressure on the federal government."

The hero-worship would only intensify. In May, Cuomo had the cover of *Rolling Stone*. In June, *Vanity Fair*. His secretary of state, the once-anonymous Melissa DeRosa, posed on the June cover of *Harper's Bazaar*. Cuomo was, for a moment at least, a rival not just to all other politicians but to pop stars too. His regular appearances on the national cable networks would inevitably bring him to his brother's show, where the two would exchange offbeat banter and Chris, invariably, would offer praise for his brother's performance, at one time asking him, repeatedly, whether he was running for president.[59]

All of it, from a distance, could make a degree of sense: during natural or manmade disasters, executives often win praise for presenting a cool exterior and attempting to comfort the populace. After hurricanes, tornadoes, or terrorist attacks, stricken citizens hunger for guidance. Giuliani may have made the mistake of sticking his emergency management headquarters *in* the World Trade Center after the first terrorist attack in 1993, but he in no way could have prevented the September 11 attacks. New York experienced mass tragedy and he was the person millions turned to for leadership.

A virus, though, was not like a terrorist attack. Executive decisions and strong, clear communication could save lives. On March 19, two days after Cuomo had rejected de Blasio's call for a shelter-in-place order for New York City, there were nearly 4,000 confirmed coronavirus cases in the five boroughs. Twenty-six people were dead. De Blasio publicly pled with Trump to send medical supplies, warning the city could run out in two to three weeks. The Thursday press conference was the first de Blasio delivered without reporters present—a precautionary measure that Cuomo would never take through the worst months of the pandemic.[60]

The next day, March 20—three full days after de Blasio's call—Cuomo said New York City, as well as the rest of the state, would shelter-in-place. But Cuomo would not call it that. It was his idea and his announcement. New York State, he said, would go on PAUSE, an acronym of his own invention: Policies Assure Uniform Safety for Everyone. All nonessential workers had to stay home. All nonessential businesses had to close and all gatherings were canceled. Anyone 70 or older had to remain at home except for solitary exercise, wear masks in the presence of others, and check the temperatures of any essential visitors and aides. All other contact was prohibited. Cuomo called this "Matilda's Law," for his own 88-year-old mother.[61]

Among de Blasio's aides, there was the widespread belief that Cuomo had delayed a shelter-in-place order because de Blasio, his perpetual political nemesis, had suggested it first. Taking action shortly after de Blasio's own declaration would have meant *following* a lower-ranked, less prestigious official in a time of crisis, and that was unforgivable in Cuomo's orbit. Better the virus keep spreading than Cuomo, fully in command, appear weak.

PAUSE would formally go into effect on Sunday, March 22 at 8:00 p.m.

"These are not helpful hints," Cuomo stressed. "These are legal provisions, they will be enforced, there will be a civil fine and mandatory closure for any business that's not in compliance."

When reporters pressed him on why the announcement was being made now and not days sooner—as of that Friday,

New York City had more than 5,000 infections, an increase of nearly 1,200 overnight—Cuomo rejected the premise that he was following the lead of anyone, either de Blasio or officials in California. PAUSE was almost identical to Newsom's shelter-in-place directive, but Cuomo said, against all available logic, it wasn't. "It is not a shelter-in-place order," Cuomo insisted. "First of all, words matter, California does not have a shelter-in-place order, they put in a new policy, it is not shelter-in-place. This is why words matter, because people are scared and people panic. Shelter-in-place is used currently for an active shooter or a school shooting."

Cuomo was referring to California's subtle rhetorical shift from shelter-in-place to "stay at home," which wasn't terminology Cuomo was using anyway. But what difference did it really make? Why not do PAUSE days earlier? Why risk so many lives? In his memoir, Cuomo argued that New Yorkers were not quite ready for such drastic measures, even if their mayor and other officials had called for them already. "The 'closedown' strategies, theoretically, could do just that: reduce activity and reduce the spread. But it wasn't that simple. Pundits will say in hindsight that we should have closed earlier. But they are missing an important point."

The point, Cuomo wrote, was that government "can announce drastic and dramatic policies to close down and reduce activity. The intelligent question was, would people follow them? It is naïve to think that government could order the most dramatic behavior changes in modern history and assume all people would salute and follow the order."

"This is not China," Cuomo continued. "This government has no ability to enforce closedown rules on 19.5 million people." He worried about measures that would lead to "panicking" and blamed the differing messages between himself and Trump that could feed public confusion. "I had to first earn the trust of the public and gain unprecedented credibility to overcome intense politics and mixed messages of the time ... California had fifty days to socialize the notion of a shutdown to the public after its first case. That was a long time. I didn't have that luxury. I would need to move faster."[62]

Cuomo was referring to the appearance of California's first coronavirus case in late January. But Newsom and other leaders hadn't spent fifty days "socializing" the populace to the idea of schools, businesses, and sporting events being entirely shut down. As recently as March 15, five days before PAUSE was announced in New York, Newsom was straining to keep restaurants open. "We don't believe, ultimately" that calling for a statewide closure "is necessary at this moment," Newsom said that day. "We are asking that restaurants practice deep social distancing by reducing occupancy by half."[63] But he and other local officials moved quickly, the next day, to close down San Francisco and neighboring counties, realizing economic considerations could only mean so much as coronavirus rapidly spread.

At the same juncture, both California and Washington did far more in March to prepare their residents for the inevitability

of COVID-19 disrupting everyday life. Schools closed first, telecommuting happened sooner. There were no public clashes
between Inslee and Constantine in Washington or Newsom
and Breed in California; local and statewide officials functioned
in total coordination. In his memoir, Cuomo at times portrays
himself as an almost passive actor, one of the sideline pundits he
often derides. Couldn't the governor of New York have done
far more, even in early March, to "socialize" New Yorkers to
the idea of coronavirus greatly changing their lives? As late as
March 11, when the NBA postponed their season and Trump
spoke from the Oval Office, Cuomo asked for "perspective,"
likening COVID-19 to the flu. Eight days later, on March 19,
Cuomo was still delusional enough to claim "the fear and panic
is, if anything, worse than the virus" when the numbers of cases
statewide had soared beyond 5,000.[64]

There was a greater unreality to Cuomo's claims. Californians
complied readily with the shelter-in-place order, even though it
didn't seem possible a week or two prior. Workplaces shuttered,
mass transit emptied out, and most stayed home. No evidence
exists that New Yorkers on March 17 or March 18 wouldn't have
done the same. Cuomo, however, did not apparently believe this.
He also argued, publicly at least and contrary to evidence, he had
more foresight than leaders in Washington state or California.
"In the end, we did what many thought was impossible, faster
than any government had done it at the time, and faster and
more effectively than any of the experts thought we could."[65]

It's unclear what experts Cuomo is referring to in his memoir. They are not named or cited. This may be because they did not exist in any great number at all. In interviews, the public health experts who followed New York's response to COVID-19 agreed that the delayed action to close down the city and restrict movement led to an early and extraordinary death toll.

In April, Dr. Tom Frieden, the former head of the CDC and the New York City Health Department, estimated that if New York had adopted widespread social distancing measures a week or two earlier, the death toll from the coronavirus outbreak might have been reduced by 50 to 80 percent.[66]

At the time, with the pandemic so new, no modeling had yet been made public to support Frieden's analysis, though it hewed to scientific consensus. In late May, scientists at Columbia University's Mailman School of Public Health released a study finding that if social distancing had been in place in major American metropolitan areas one to two weeks earlier, more than half of the infections and deaths seen to date could have been prevented.

In the New York metropolitan area, the study found that 209,987 or 80 percent of confirmed cases and 17,514 or 80 percent of deaths could have been avoided if the same sequence of shutdown orders had been applied one week earlier. Had they come two weeks earlier, a reduction of 246,082 cases (94 percent) and 20,427 deaths (94 percent) could have occurred in the New York metropolitan area.[67]

"Here we are in New York and we kind of dithered in early March, we didn't act aggressively enough," said lead researcher Jeffrey Shaman, a professor of environmental health sciences at Columbia. "It was a lack of recognition to understand the threat was really here."[68]

The month following Cuomo's belated implementation of a shutdown order would be, perhaps, the very worst in New York City's history. Most residents huddled indoors, terrified that the very air they breathed could be rife with a virus they hardly understood. Sirens began to split open the day and night, 911 calls reaching a pitch never before seen. Those still forced to leave their homes to work—the medical professionals, the supermarket clerks, the subway conductors and bus drivers, the sanitation workers—endured the daily dread of interacting with human beings in confined spaces, the virus everywhere.

A profound divide emerged between the white-collar professionals safely curled behind laptop screens at home and the city's vast working class, those tasked with sustaining what was left of a dying metropolis. "It's frightening," said Terence Layne, a Manhattan driver, describing operating a bus in early April. "Every morning I leave my home and I ask myself, Is this the day? Is this the day I become contaminated and infected?"[69]

Hospitals, particularly the ailing public institutions, were quickly overwhelmed, as nurses and doctors struggled to contain the surge of bodies and treat those who were fighting through their last breaths. Shortages of personal protective equipment were so dire that nurses at one Manhattan hospital resorted to wearing trash bags.[70]

At Elmhurst, a 545-bed public hospital in Queens, conditions were apocalyptic. Though Cuomo and de Blasio were racing to increase hospital capacity, eventually creating makeshift facilities at the Jacob Javits Convention Center and the USTA Billie Jean King National Tennis Center, neighborhood hospitals at the epicenter of the pandemic did not have the staff and the beds to manage what the virus had brought to their doors. Doctors and nurses struggled to secure ventilators, then the most available life-saving treatment. Patients died in emergency rooms while waiting for beds. Outside, a refrigerated truck was stationed to hold the bodies of the dead, the hospital morgue filled. Those in the neighborhood who wanted to get tested would up line as early as 6:00 a.m., only to wait all day or at 6:00 a.m. to then wait all day.[71]

When Cuomo and de Blasio each boasted about New York's healthcare system in early March, now a lifetime ago for the suffering, they predictably omitted its greatest failings. In the city and surrounding counties, the system existed as a patchwork of public and private hospitals, the gulf between them enormous. Some private hospitals in Manhattan and elsewhere enjoyed lavish funding, thanks to the attention of extraordinarily wealthy donors and an affluent, well-insured base of patients. Public hospitals, perpetually cash-strapped, treated the city's poorest residents, many of them Medicaid recipients. Even when the economy was strong, these institutions never had sufficient resources—and there were a lot fewer of them than there used to be, especially in disadvantaged neighborhoods.

In late March, the window to contain coronavirus long closed and the PAUSE order in full effect, Cuomo intoned often about hospital capacity. Across New York State, there were 53,000 beds, and in certain parts of the city, they were rapidly filling up. Cuomo began holding press briefings at the Javits Center, the temporary 1,000-bed site on the Far West Side of Manhattan, which in a normal year hosted an auto show, a comic-con, a book convention, and various other large events.

By the end of March, at least 1,550 people had died of COVID-19 statewide. There were a staggering 75,795 confirmed cases.

"This is going to crash the healthcare system," Cuomo said.

CARNAGE

Far Rockaway is a working-class neighborhood on the eastern point of the Rockaway peninsula, near the border of Nassau County. With a high concentration of public housing, the Queens community can feel both close-knit and isolated, edged against the Atlantic Ocean, far away from the glittering city center.

For many years, two hospitals served the peninsula: St. John's Episcopal Hospital and Peninsula Hospital. In 2012, only a year into his term, Cuomo moved quickly to shut down Peninsula, a 173-bed hospital. Though the hospital didn't always enjoy the best reputation, residents passionately rallied to save it as the Department of Health readied to shut it down.

"As a child, I was raised by my grandma and she'd always take me there when I needed care," local Iris Delgado said in 2011. "That's where my children went to the emergency room when they broke their arms and needed stitches. When I was diagnosed with cancer, I had my chemo and surgery there. They were so good to me, holding my hand, making me feel at home."[72]

Peninsula was an easy target because it had filed for bankruptcy and its lab failed a state exam. The State Department of Health rejected Peninsula's plan to fix their lab. Without a functioning lab, Peninsula was effectively hamstrung, unable to perform a vast majority of services like blood tests or transfusions. Since it served a poor, Medicaid-dependent populace, Peninsula did not make money. Under Cuomo, its fate was sealed.

After Peninsula's closure, the controversy faded, though Superstorm Sandy would soon batter the Rockaways, ruining homes and leaving thousands without power. When there's no crisis, it's easy to forget about hospitals or even regard them as anachronisms—why have such large buildings waiting with empty rooms and beds? Absent a major terrorist attack, which hadn't come in almost two decades, austerity-minded executives like Cuomo could marshal public sentiment to their side when deciding to close hospitals. Sure, the local neighborhood would complain, but people would eventually move on. The Rockaway Peninsula still had one hospital. It would make do well enough, the state assumed.

In March, like the Atlantic tides under Superstorm Sandy eight years earlier, coronavirus ripped through Far Rockaway. In dire need of ventilators, St. John's Episcopal, the lone 257-bed hospital left on the peninsula, was quickly deluged with patients overflowing into the hallways. Even staff were testing positive with the virus.[73] One nurse described a night, early in the pandemic, when 10 people died right in front of her.[74]

Teeming with public housing and nursing homes, and filled with residents who did not have the luxury of performing work remotely, Far Rockaway became an epicenter of the pandemic in New York City—and therefore, in those dark early days, the world. In May, when New York City finally tallied its death toll by neighborhood, Far Rockway was revealed to have at least 340 deaths per 100,000 people, nearly twice the city average of 175. Learning of the numbers, a local city council member broke down in tears. "There's a lot more we could have done earlier," he said.[75]

★ ★ ★

How much life could a second hospital have saved? There's no way to know an exact number. What did become clear, though, was that cities and countries with larger hospital capacity were able to blunt the worst effects of the pandemic early on. In Germany, where politicians would rail against the high number of hospital beds in better times, the sheer number of hospitals allowed officials to efficiently isolate and treat the infected during the pandemic's first wave. "In contrast to Spain, France, and Italy, we have a very high density of hospitals and beds, and this has emerged as a big advantage in this crisis," explained Uwe Janssens, head of the German Interdisciplinary Association for Intensive Care and Emergency Medicine.[76]

The pandemic would reveal, in the most plain and brutal ways, the inequity baked into New York's healthcare system. It would shine a harsh light on a two decade-long trend that Cuomo aided and abetted at every turn, one that would prove deadly in March and April: the mass closure of hospitals.

In 2000, there were 73,931 licensed hospital beds in New York State. Twenty years later, as COVID-19 killed tens of thousands, there were just 53,000.[77] The losses were endured everywhere, but struck working-class neighborhoods in New York City especially hard. Queens, the original epicenter of the virus, lost at least five hospitals over that stretch. In total, at least 28 hospitals shut their doors across the state since 2000, according to the New York State Nurses Association.[78]

Twenty years on, another particularly fatal statistic loomed: New York City, per capita, had among the worst intensive care unit capacities in America, trailing cities such as Chicago, Detroit, Fort Lauderdale, Baltimore, Nashville, and Las Vegas.[79]

The hospital closures took off in 2006, under Republican Governor George Pataki. That year, a state-sponsored commissioner recommended closing more than 20 hospitals and shrinking and merging dozens of others to save money. Some of this was a function of national trends—hospitals are large and expensive, and smaller outpatient facilities were prioritized.

But bureaucrats in New York approached shuttering hospitals with particular zeal. Stephen Berger, an investment banker, chaired the commission, and would later join Cuomo's administration in 2011. Two years later, Berger argued that *more* New York hospitals needed to close, writing that "allowing hospitals that have outlived their usefulness to close is a necessary step in the transformation of our healthcare system." The safety-net hospitals serving the city's poor were bleeding too much money, he argued, and couldn't be sustained anymore, especially with the rise of community-based primary care.[80]

In 2013, the Cuomo administration approved the closure of the 500-bed Long Island College Hospital in Brooklyn over loud community protest. "Andrew Cuomo has repeatedly stated, over and over again, that New York has excess capacity of hospital beds, that it's too expensive and not needed and we need to reduce spending. He said this over and over again throughout his entire tenure," said Sean Petty, a pediatric nurse at a public hospital in the Bronx and a high-ranking member of the state's politically-active nurses union, NYSNA.[81]

In 2018, Cuomo announced a proposal to merge three Brooklyn hospitals to boost preventive and primary care services, and to rehabilitate the three facilities while streamlining their electronic records system. More than 200 beds at Kingsbrook, one of the three hospitals, were targeted for elimination.

The group tasked with designing the consolidation plan was the hospital network, Northwell Health—specifically, its consulting arm, Northwell Ventures. The result was a new network, One Brooklyn Health, created to oversee the hospitals. The chairman of the network's board of directors is Alexander Rovt, a billionaire Donald Trump supporter who had funneled hundreds of thousands of dollars to Cuomo's campaigns.

Julie Keefe, a Kingsbrook nurse and organizer, lamented that political pushback against the proposal had been relatively muted. "Local politicians and unions have been afraid to go against Cuomo on this plan and afraid of retaliation," she said. "They once saw it as a political death sentence."[82]

Mostly mum was the Greater New York Hospital Association, the nonprofit advocacy group representing more than 200 hospitals across the state, including the wealthiest private networks. Beyond real estate and Wall Street, there may not have been a more influential lobby in New York—or one with closer ties to Cuomo. The co-chair of Cuomo's latest Medicaid Redesign Team was Michael Dowling, the CEO of Northwell Health, perhaps GNYHA's most powerful member. Dowling was close to father and son: he had once served as Mario Cuomo's deputy secretary and director of Health, Education, and Human Services.

Dowling was often at Cuomo junior's side, publicly and privately, along with Kenneth Raske, GNYHA's president. Cuomo's public schedule for March 2020 showed him speaking to or meeting with Raske at least seven times.

That month, catastrophe reigned. Some patients were too sick to be transferred between overwhelmed hospitals. Squabbling between the Cuomo and de Blasio administrations contributed to an uncoordinated effort. Overburdened hospitals too often mixed infected patients with the uninfected, spreading coronavirus to non-COVID-19 units. State, city government, and hospital officials kept shifting guidelines about when exposed and ill frontline workers should return to work. While Cuomo focused attention on procuring ventilators, hospitals lacked critical resources including oxygen, vital-signs monitors, and dialysis machines.[83]

Cuomo, as the governor of New York State, had near-total control over which hospitals survived and which did not. He certified whether they could continue to operate. Enthusiastically implementing his predecessor's hospital-closure agenda, Cuomo had also spent much of his time in office attempting to cut Medicaid spending, particularly to the cash-strapped public hospitals in New York City.

Medicaid was a lifeline for so-called safety net hospitals, the public institutions serving the urban poor in the five boroughs and the rural poor in the northern and western reaches of the state. Struggling for support in ordinary times, they were verging on collapse in the early months of the pandemic.

Berger, the investment banker who oversaw the commission recommending hospital shutdowns in the 2000s, joined Cuomo in 2011 to oversee his first Medicaid Redesign Team, which was tasked with slashing funding for Medicaid in Cuomo's first term. Cuomo successfully shrunk Medicaid reimbursements, damaging the financially fragile healthcare facilities serving low-income patients. Public hospitals like Jacobi and Lincoln in the Bronx, Elmhurst in Queens, and Kings County Hospital in Brooklyn were on the frontlines of the pandemic, treating the poorest and the sickest patients.

In early 2020, before COVID-19 appeared in New York, the state had been facing a $6 billion budget hole due to rising Medicaid costs. Despite Cuomo's best efforts, Medicaid had consumed more of the state budget since the Affordable Care Act boosted enrollment in New York. Some of the budget gap, though, was Cuomo's own making: postponing Medicaid payments and failing in the past to iron out inefficiencies like the state paying Medicaid costs for relatively wealthy, private hospitals that don't need the aid in the first place.

Before the pandemic hit, Cuomo wanted to slash Medicaid spending once more, in part to close the gap. While left-leaning lawmakers proposed tax increases on the wealthy to raise the necessary funds, Cuomo rejected the idea out of hand. What startled Democrats in the state legislature, though, was Cuomo's *insistence* on Medicaid cuts even as COVID-19 spread and public hospitals, so dependent on this assistance, were the last line of defense against a full-scale collapse of the city. The pandemic had not changed Cuomo's calculus at all: the hospitals needed to suffer because the budget would have to be balanced, and tax increases were off the table. How much would hospitals lose? At least $400 million.

Members of the Medicaid Redesign Team—particularly those who opposed the pending cuts—recalled that Dowling was in near-total control, along with Robert Mujica, Cuomo's budget director and an ex-officio member. The team largely existed to rubberstamp whatever proposal came from Dowling and Mujica.

One state senator, speaking for many Democrats in the chamber, called the proposed cuts "obscene" and "immoral."[84] Cuomo was prepared to make them anyway.

★ ★ ★

One of the great fonts of Cuomo's power was the state budget. It was a place where his control was great, almost total. A new budget would be adopted in the middle of the worst pandemic in a hundred years. Unlike many other states and cities, New York State always began its fiscal year in April, not July. The passing of the state budget overlapped fully with the legislative session, which extended from January through June. Cuomo's predecessors were willing to accept budgets that were not "on-time"— passed after April 1. But Cuomo, hungry to burnish his image as a competent taskmaster, had long been obsessed with hitting that deadline, even if the budgets ultimately did not deliver on ambitious or far-reaching priorities. What they did usually deliver on, however, was whatever he wanted in a particular year. By default, it was almost impossible for a budget to disappoint Cuomo.

Those who followed national politics were used to a tug-of-war between the president and Congress. Often, it could seem like Congress had even more influence than the president, especially when power is divided between the parties. Albany did not function that way—at least not in the 21st century. When Cuomo's father, Mario, enacted his first budget in 1983, he showed up uninvited at the chambers of the Democrat-controlled State Assembly. The speaker, Stanley Fink, asked him to say a few words.

"I gave you a budget," the elder Cuomo said. "You gave me back a better one." The chamber burst into applause.

Thirty-seven years on, such a balance of power had evaporated. Every March, Cuomo and the legislative leaders of each chamber negotiated the titanic state budget, accounting for more than $170 billion in spending. Funding levels determined the quality of schools, transportation, the environment, roadways, and just about every other entity, large and small, throughout the state. Unrelated policy matters—in 2019, for example, the ban on plastic bags as well as the implementation of a congestion pricing system—were often rammed into the omnibus budget bill.

Andrew Cuomo was at his most dominant during budget negotiations because New York's constitution and subsequent court rulings allowed him to be: once Cuomo introduced his version of the budget, legislators could only strike out or reduce spending items. Adding items of their own was very difficult. Additional spending items had to be set aside separately and were subject to the governor's veto. In a decade, the legislature had never successfully overrode a Cuomo veto. This had always made his proposed budget much more of the final word than either of the one-house budgets offered by the Senate or Assembly.

Cuomo and the leaders of the two legislative bodies, the Senate majority leader and Assembly speaker, hashed out the budget largely out of public view. With little time to spare— sometimes just a few hours—lawmakers attempted to read, with the help of weary staff, thousands of pages. The enormous, discordant document was difficult to reject, even with poison pills, since voting against it meant shooting down necessary funding for schools, hospitals, and public transportation. Starry-eyed first-term legislators were often disillusioned by how opaque and retrograde lawmaking can be in New York's capital. The mechanics of it, over the course of a century, had changed little.

"It's worthy of Vladimir Putin and the Saudi government," fumed a former state assembly member. "It's absurd and bad and at the heart of Albany dysfunction."[85]

State lawmakers had begun 2020 huddled in Albany, though the pandemic was making that a dangerous proposition. Several legislators had already tested positive for coronavirus. For the first time, the budget would be largely negotiated over the phone and videoconference, with lawmakers returning to the chamber to cast their votes. The State Capitol, abuzz with lobbyists and protesters and curious onlookers in a normal year, was closed to the public. After a celebratory 2019, in which Democrats controlled both chambers of the legislature for the first time in a decade, an unsettling silence gripped the building. The virus, most assumed, was lurking everywhere.

As the clock ticked down to April 1, Cuomo had one burning priority that was never discussed at his much-celebrated coronavirus press briefings: legal immunity for hospitals and nursing homes. Just days earlier, on March 25, Cuomo's Department of Health had issued a directive ordering nursing homes to accept patients infected with COVID-19 who were discharged from hospitals but could be convalescing.[86]

Operators warned that such a policy could worsen the spread of the virus, which was already speeding through nursing homes in New York City. Nursing homes had struggled to limit outbreaks of coronavirus because of their large staffs that came and went so often. Admitting sick COVID-19 patients seemed to be a needless and heightened risk. One explanation for the policy, later offered by Cuomo, was that the state was worried about hospital capacity—though the excess beds built out could have temporarily hosted nursing home patients discharged from hospitals.

Immunity would shield these healthcare institutions from inevitable lawsuits as the death toll mounted and some families of the deceased blamed nursing homes for lax oversight of their loved ones. In Washington, the Republican Senate majority leader, Mitch McConnell, would fight ferociously for such provisions, angering Democrats across America. The language of the immunity bill the Republicans hoped to pass shared striking similarities with Cuomo's law in New York.

Once more, Cuomo and right-wing Republicans were in sync, but most mainstream media outlets and liberal pundits were unwilling to make such a connection.

Powerful interests wanted the immunity provision in the state budget and Cuomo was happy to oblige. Lobbyists from the Greater New York Hospital Association helped write and insert the language into the state budget, lawmakers close to the process recalled. GNYHA long enjoyed a deep relationship to Cuomo, as one of the largest donors to the State Democratic Party, which Cuomo controlled, and to Cuomo's own campaign.

For those watching closely, it was becoming clear that Cuomo was farming out much of his pandemic-response policy to the hospital association, Dowling and Raske in particular. Longtime allies of Cuomo, they would chart the direction of the next year. Dennis Whalen, a Northwell lobbyist, would slide into the Department of Health to oversee policy decisions. Whalen was typical of the revolving door within the Cuomo administration: before his lobbying days, he had served in state government.

GNYHA had "more access than most people in the entire government," said State Senator Alessandra Biaggi, a Bronx Democrat. "They have essentially been given carte blanche for our legislative process."

Cuomo got his wish. When the trimmed down budget passed in April, the immunity provision—officially the Emergency Disaster Treatment Protection Act—was tucked inside, one tiny sliver of the usual megalith. The provision was so sweeping that it covered virtually all lawsuits, even those unrelated to coronavirus. A patient recovering from a broken leg or a heart attack would be unable to bring a medical malpractice lawsuit, as long as a state of emergency was declared.

Legislative leaders deserved blame for failing to stand up to Cuomo and allowing healthcare lobbyists to write a bill granting the industry such unprecedented protections. Rank-and-file lawmakers were only dimly aware of what was happening, so focused on fighting off Medicaid cuts and attempting to secure protections for tenants facing evictions. Among legislators, it was the most dispiriting budget negotiation in memory.

"This budget, this values document, makes a terrible statement that we value big businesses and profits more than we value people, our people, the people of this state, and that is simply not who we are," said one Manhattan lawmaker.[87]

Ron Kim, a state assembly member who was strongly critical of the immunity provision, said that state legislators didn't even know it existed until days after the budget had been passed. Written into the budget near the deadline, and considered non-negotiable by Cuomo's office, it was not explained at all to most lawmakers—only legislative leaders were aware of it, and kept it quiet for fear the body could shoot down the budget altogether.

"I thought it was criminal that this happened," Kim said. "To find out a Democratic governor in a Democratic state would put something in like this—we knew that Governor Cuomo was pro-corporate but for this to happen in a budget, I was literally in shock for forty-eight hours. I couldn't believe this actually happened."[88]

Cuomo wasn't done. In addition to the immunity provision, he had won yet another emergency power from the budget process, one that could make him as close to a monarch as any democratically-elected executive could be: the near-unilateral ability, over the course of the next year, to slash the state budget. Particularly, it would be Cuomo's budget director, Robert Mujica, deciding what to gut and when.

Mujica had been a longtime staffer for the State Senate Republicans until Cuomo plucked him for his current role, which became one of the most significant in the state. Like

Cuomo, Mujica had an aversion to raising taxes and a skepticism of progressive policy goals.

Both men embraced austerity. If Mujica determined revenues had not met projections and the budget needed balancing, he could order cuts on his own. All the legislature could do is counter with their suggested reductions. If the legislature didn't come up with a counter-proposal in 10 days, Mujica's cuts would become official. Lawmakers were not allowed, under these new rules, to suggest additions to the budget or revenue raisers.

All of these budget negotiations transpired beyond the consciousness of the Cuomo-adoring public. The enormous, society-altering death tolls did not weaken his image or dent his polling numbers. Cuomo's favorability rating, once so middling, hit 77 percent at the end of April.[89] It was a tale of two realities. In one, a commanding Cuomo appeared daily at his briefings and on cable television to tout the state's progress as pundits largely praised him for taming coronavirus while Trump allowed it to spread, unchecked. Fans had begun selling Cuomo-themed merchandise online. Several, including the TV host Ellen DeGeneres, began calling themselves "Cuomosexuals."

"Whatever his political future, Cuomo has become a trusted voice in a world of uncertainty," wrote *Rolling Stone* in April. "His homely PowerPoint slides are routinely memed. The slow, booming cadence of his sentences, once grating, could probably be marketed as a meditation app if we end up surviving this thing."[90]

The other reality, taking shape in the nursing homes and hospitals of New York City, was one of unfathomable catastrophe.

At one nursing home in Brooklyn, the 360-bed Cobble Hill Health Center, more people died by the end of April than in the entire city of San Francisco.

Elderly residents spent their final moments crying out for oxygen that never came. A woman on a nebulizer slumped out of bed and hit her head on the ground, where she remained for over thirty minutes, begging for help. Nurses, lacking personal protective equipment, wore kitchen aprons and trash bags, fearing they would soon collapse and die. There was little effort to separate the patients with obvious respiratory symptoms from those who hadn't yet caught the virus. As staff sickened, operators could barely procure coronavirus tests.

The nursing home repeatedly begged the State Department of Health and the NYC Office of Emergency Management for more supplies, even asking whether patients could be sent to the makeshift hospital at the Javits Center. The request was denied. "If our governor really wanted to help, he would have first protected the nursing homes," said Mina Clarke, a 37-year-old patient who had been recovering from a major orthopedic surgery at Cobble Hill when COVID-19 hit.[91]

Cuomo was blunt: it was not the state's responsibility to send more personal protective equipment to nursing homes. The deaths, initially, did not change his thinking at all. "We have been helping them with more PPE but, again, it's not our job," Cuomo said in late April.

Fifty-five people alone would die at Cobble Hill. It was one epicenter of the epicenter, a hellscape among many. The numbers, in that period, could be numbing. In a city where less than 400 people were murdered in a single year, more than 500 were dying per day. On average, statewide, as many as 10,000 new cases appeared on one day.

Deaths were not only occurring at healthcare facilities. Long before they reached hospitals, New Yorkers were dying in their apartments, gasping through broken breaths. On April 14, New York City's Health Department made a crucial decision: they were now including, in their death count, people who had never tested positive for the virus but were presumed to have died of it.

Given the scarcity of testing, this was a logical decision, since public health experts always presumed the toll coronavirus was taking to be far higher. The city's death toll, with the new count, officially reached 10,000.[92]

* * *

Cuomo had been wrong, of course. The fear was not worse than the virus. The virus was killing far more than was ever feared a month earlier. For the rest of the pandemic, New York City's Health Department would maintain a more precise metric, counting deaths of both those who tested positive for coronavirus and those presumed to have had it. Cuomo's Health Department, however, refused to recognize the city's count, publishing their own data. Each day, New York City and New York State would announce different counts of those who died from COVID-19, with Cuomo's government consistently posting a lower number. Later in the summer, Cuomo's office would even ask the Centers for Disease Control to stop reporting New York City's probable death numbers.

In the early months of the pandemic, New York's death toll, with much of it concentrated in the city and surrounding suburbs, could account for as much as a quarter of the nation's total. At the tail end of April and into May, caseloads finally declined, thanks in part to the strict lockdown New York had finally been placed under. For Cuomo, this was a victory, the mass death less meaningful than the trajectory itself. Months later, at the end of June, Cuomo unveiled an enormous foam mountain at one of his press conferences, physically manifesting the downward curve in cases.

"We paid the price and we dealt with that spike and we climbed right up the mountain," Cuomo intoned. "We got smart. New Yorkers stepped up. We wore masks. We socially distanced. We closed down. And we stopped the curve. We plateaued."

By the time of the mountain's unveiling, almost 25,000 people had died statewide of COVID-19.

Numbers were always a challenge for the Cuomo administration. They were tabulated in curious ways, obscured in others. City and state death tolls could never sync up. And no one—not healthcare experts, journalists, or politicians—could figure out just how many people died in the state's many nursing homes.

Nursing homes, nationwide, were a breeding ground for coronavirus. New York was not alone in discharging patients who had the virus already into homes. New York was not the only state to struggle with testing or the allocation of necessary protective equipment. But Cuomo, again, stood apart in the unusual, misleading way his state accounted for just how many people died there. Officially, according to state statistics, around 6,500 nursing home residents died by the late summer. That number was large, though it didn't represent anything close to a majority of the more than 37,000 deaths overall.

The trouble with such a figure was who was included and who wasn't. If a nursing home resident was infected with coronavirus in the facility and later died there, the State Department of Health recorded it as part of its nursing home death tally. But a nursing home resident who contracted the virus in the facility and died at a hospital—many residents exhibiting symptoms were naturally transferred to hospitals—would not be part of the tally. This neglected an unknown number of residents, potentially thousands, who were infected within nursing homes.

As Cuomo gained acclaim for his response to coronavirus, a small group of people began to push back against the prevailing narrative: families of those who died in nursing homes. Many, as they said in interviews, had been admirers of the governor, among those comforted when he took to the television in the early days of the pandemic. Now they were devastated, angry, and confused, seeking answers where there didn't seem to be any.

"I was a big Cuomo fan prior to all of this," said Alexa Rivera, a Brooklyn resident whose 78-year-old mother was infected in a Long Island nursing home and died in a nearby hospital. "I thought he was bold in his statements and how he expressed himself. But when you give someone a get out of jail free card, it makes it easier for them to do the bare minimum."[93]

Rivera started a group called VoicesforSeniors to help advocate for families who lost relatives and friends in nursing homes. She said her mother was at a nursing home to recover from knee surgery when her health deteriorated, though staffers initially told her that her mother would be discharged. Information about her condition, she said, was sorely lacking.

April Reese had a similar experience with her 79-year-old father, who contracted coronavirus in another Long Island nursing home. Through tears, Reese recounted how her father, once robust, suddenly grew sick, coughing constantly. A nursing home staffer told her he received a chest X-ray that came back negative.

Later, her father informed her he had never had a chest X-ray at all. He was given amoxicillin, a treatment for stomach ulcers, when he was clearly exhibiting COVID-19 symptoms.

"The administration in that nursing home, the way they treated me and my father, it was a shame," Reese said.[94]

Her father would be transferred to a nearby hospital where he eventually died. Though both Reese and Rivera's parents were infected in nursing homes, neither of their deaths were actually counted in the State Department of Health's nursing homes death tally because they were transported to hospitals. Instead, both were simply recorded as hospital deaths.

Among states that counted nursing home deaths as a separate category—some didn't at all—no state had chosen to exclude residents who died at hospitals from their tallies. On April 13, New York started reporting nursing home deaths as a separate category. At that moment, they counted only confirmed deaths, not presumed deaths. Hospital transfer deaths—residents moved from homes to hospitals—were counted too.

On May 3, with little explanation, presumed nursing home deaths *were* included in the tally but hospital transfers were dropped. The nursing home total would jump because of the presumed deaths, helping to disguise the significance of what had just happened. As the spring wore on and the death toll in nursing homes kept climbing, families of the dead, advocates, and politicians in both parties grew alarmed that no accurate tally could ever be produced. After all, didn't most nursing home operators in the earliest days want to transfer sick residents to hospitals whenever possible, whether to save their lives or avoid a death on their property?

The questions, at first, came from conservatives. Among Republicans wearying of Cuomo's enormous popularity—he was a Democrat, after all, and some unfounded speculation had begun to crop up that he could replace the wobbly Joe Biden as the nominee for president—the nursing home issue was easy to seize on.

Unlike Cuomo's indefensible delay of a shelter-in-place order for New York City, the mismanagement of nursing homes and the failure to report accurate data could not be linked to Trump's disastrous federal response. Cuomo could at least claim, with limited plausibility, that he would've acted sooner if the federal government took charge and told him what to do. The nursing home deaths, however, were mostly a local matter, though Cuomo tried to indict Trump on this as well, arguing the state was merely following CDC guidance, even though the federal agency warned nursing homes to keep coronavirus out of their facilities, adding that homes could admit coronavirus patients only if they could properly care for them.

"Cuomo killed grandma" became a rallying cry on the right, heard on Fox and in conservative social media circles. But those gathering against Cuomo outside his Midtown office were not far right provocateurs. They were families of the dead, seeking justice. They wanted to know how and why their mothers and fathers and sisters and brothers had died. They wanted to understand why these deaths were lost in the tally or, more simply, why the state made the decision to discharge coronavirus patients back into their facilities. And they had allies on the left: Democratic legislators in the Assembly and State Senate were beginning to call for outside, independent investigations into the nursing home debacle, with thousands dead and no true way to account for all of them.

In a tacit acknowledgment that the hospital transfer policy was a failure, Cuomo announced on May 10 that residents could only go back to their facilities if they tested negative for coronavirus. But the issue, for Cuomoworld, would always be framed through a blatantly partisan lens: it didn't really matter because Republicans cared about it.

"By early spring, Republicans needed an offense to distract from the narrative of their botched federal response—and they needed it badly," Cuomo wrote. "So they decided to attack Democratic governors and blame them for nursing home deaths." Though much reporting focused on the fact that his prior policy had been "rescinded," this was not quite the case. A separate guidance was issued to hospitals, stopping them from sending patients to nursing homes while the March 25 memo was yanked from the internet altogether. Zucker, Cuomo's health commissioner, would later testify that the policy technically remained in effect.

Media coverage, as it often did, fell on Cuomo's side. "NEW RULES ON NURSING HOMES. Cuomo: Hospitals Can't Discharge Patients to Care Facilities Unless They Test Negative for Virus," came a headline from *Newsday*, the only daily newspaper serving Nassau and Suffolk counties, large suburbs of New York City.

Missing was Cuomo's role in the catastrophe. The *Newsday* headline left the impression that nursing homes or hospitals created a dubious policy that Cuomo had now reversed. It was entirely unclear who enforced the old rules. The reader was left to wonder if hospitals or nursing homes did. The second sentence in the headline implied, wrongly, that hospitals were willingly dispatching nursing home residents who tested positive for coronavirus back to their nursing homes. Hospitals were being *compelled* to send them and nursing homes were *ordered* to take them.

Who did the compelling and the ordering? Andrew Cuomo, the governor of New York, who controlled the Department of Health.

Beyond nursing homes, home healthcare attendants were mobilizing against the Cuomo administration, faulting the governor for failing to enforce an executive order that required employers to provide safe working conditions during COVID-19. Attendants said their agencies had not provided them with adequate personal protective equipment and many had been forced to work 24-hour workdays for only 13 hours' pay.

More than 700 home attendants signed a letter contending that Cuomo continues "to disregard our health and the health of the patients we care for, treating us as expendable."

Brigida Bautista, a home attendant from the Bronx, recalled that her agency only gave her 10 masks for 15 days, when she has to bathe, feed, and clean two elderly patients who, she feared, could transfer the virus to her.

"The governor doesn't really care about us," Bautista, who speaks Spanish, said through a translator. "How many home care workers have already died? Cuomo doesn't remember home attendants."[95]

★ ★ ★

State prisons were rife with coronavirus. Releasing inmates, who were crowded into decrepit and unsanitary cell blocks, was the quickest and most obvious way to cut down on the spread of the virus.

Cuomo's reputation as a liberal in the national media did not correlate, in any serious way, to his instincts on criminal justice. From the time he took office in 2011 to the outbreak of the pandemic in March 2020, Cuomo had granted clemency to just 24 prisoners. In a far shorter span of time, the otherwise revanchist Donald Trump granted clemency to 94 people charged with federal crimes.

Cuomo lagged behind his predecessors too. His father, who completed three full terms, issued 37 commutations. Hugh Carey, another influential Democratic governor, granted 155 commutations.[96] Remarkably, Cuomo had gone his entire first term without commuting the sentence of a single person, and only relented under pressure from civil rights activists.[97]

On one hand, Cuomo would luck out: coronavirus, so widespread in New York, never ravaged prisons in his own state the way it did elsewhere. Even into February 2021, New York had a total of 1,207 cases per 10,000 inmates, a rate that placed it well behind large states like California, Texas, and Florida, which had higher rates in their prisons.[98] (California, for example, had surpassed 4,000.)

Over the course of the year, Cuomo would release more than 3,500 inmates, largely due to the pandemic. But criteria had been limited to those who had committed nonviolent offenses, shrinking the pool of possible releases and overlooking many elderly inmates who had been locked behind bars for decades. Of the 43,000 locked up in New York, at least 9,500 were over the age of 50.

"In all these cases, the governor has the absolute ability to grant clemencies, to grant compassionate release, to allow people to go home," said Katie Schaffer, the director of organizing and advocacy at the Center for Community Alternatives, a longtime reform organization. "That is entirely within his power and his discretion. He has taken wholly insufficient action."

That insufficiency extended into the new year. In 2021, a new coronavirus outbreak threatened to overrun state prisons. Hundreds of prisoners tested positive in January. Though the US Centers for Disease Control and Prevention encouraged prison officials to "vaccinate staff and incarcerated/detained persons of correctional or detention facilities at the same time because of their shared increased risk of disease," the inmate population was not among those Cuomo had listed as eligible to receive a vaccine. The Legal Aid Society called Cuomo's policy "cruel and irresponsible."

Cuomo faced renewed criticism from advocates and at least one bold-faced name: Chelsea Clinton. "We've had ~2,000 new #covid19 cases in New York State prisons in the last 6 weeks alone. Please @NYGovCuomo allow and prioritize #covid19 vaccinations of incarcerated people in our state," Clinton tweeted on January 13.[99]

Despite outbreak after outbreak, little changed around the country to mitigate the threat of the virus spreading throughout prisons. Inmates remained jammed together, sharing bathrooms, dining tables, and sleeping quarters. Opportunities to safely isolate from someone infected with the virus were virtually nonexistent.

The problem wasn't only limited to inmates. Since guards, lawyers, workers and people entering and leaving custody move between prisons and the larger community, the implications of outbreaks behind bars extend far beyond the walls of the prisons.

Cuomo did little, as infections picked up again, to create a vaccination plan for the state's prisons. By early 2021, infections behind bars in New York had climbed to nearly 9,000 since the start of the pandemic.[100]

One mother whose son fell ill from COVID-19 in an upstate prison said she was not surprised to learn he had tested positive.

"I knew this was bound to happen," she said. "I didn't think [he] would be able to save himself from it."[101]

★ ★ ★

The body count could only faze Cuomo so much. To the public, he was still the coronavirus conqueror. His favorability rating was no longer a stratospheric 77 percent, but it was still quite high, hovering at 66 percent in late May, when much of New York's colossal death toll was well known.[102] The governor's mastery of the media narrative was reminiscent of another New York strongman who helped trigger an urban crisis decades earlier.

Before Robert Caro's magnificent biography cratered his reputation for good, Robert Moses, the New York master builder, was regarded as an almost mythic figure in the city. Like Cuomo, he was the subject of fawning press. Moses's turn as a hero actually lasted far longer than most people alive today realize: he was venerated for *decades*. Imagine Cuomo t-shirts on Etsy proliferating from now until the 2060s.

Moses, like Cuomo, had true accomplishments. If anything, Moses earned at least some of his adulation, overseeing the mass construction of public parks and housing that were still in use decades after his death. His racism, and noted hatred of public transit, kept trains from running to his brilliant Long Island beaches, but the beaches still appeared from scratch. There were few highways and bridges in the New York area that didn't emerge from direct Moses action.

With the help of federal largesse, Moses, like magic, could cut the ribbon on a major infrastructure project almost every year. Though his concentration of power in the state was unprecedented—at one time, he could head up as many as a dozen city and state agencies, controlling the flow of money like no mayor or governor—his image was one of unadorned benevolence.

"The image was of the totally unselfish and altruistic public servant who wanted nothing for himself but the chance to serve," Caro wrote. "The image was of the fearless independent above politics ... The image was of the relentless foe of bureaucrats, the dynamic slasher of red tape ... The image was of the man who Got Things Done, who produced for the public tangible, visible, dramatic achievements..."[103]

In the 1920s, 30s, and 40s, few newspapers wrote critically about Moses, even as he illegally seized land, blighted once thriving neighborhoods with disruptive highways, displaced thousands of working-class residents, and undermined what had been a world-class public transportation system. New York's subway map was effectively frozen in time for almost a century because of decisions Moses made many decades earlier. Until the 1970s fiscal crisis and disinvestment in public institutions laid bare where the imperial Moses had erred, the master builder was rarely questioned.

Moses understood New York media organs would determine his public perception and, therefore, his power. He courted the press through flattery and cunning. After ribbon cuttings, he treated reporters to lavish banquets. He granted favored journalists free passes to his beaches and exemptions from tolls. If a project was especially controversial, he knew he needed to break the news first in a friendly outlet, using the corrosive power of access journalism to define his agenda in the public before opponents marshalled a response. Often, his pronouncements were treated with little analysis or scrutiny, regarded as bare fact beyond debate. Influential editorial boards always took his side.

Like Moses, Cuomo had always courted media behind the scenes with a mix of aggression and occasional flattery. He was known to call reporters personally to plead his case or yell at them, often off the record. His staff did the same.

Critics of his policies were subject to anonymous sources attacking them online or in tabloid newspapers. These anonymous sources could usually be traced back to the governor's office. Newspaper editorial boards and editors could expect calls from the governor's office when coverage wasn't to his liking.

With a decade of governing under his belt, Cuomo had become New York's preeminent political institution; since there were no term limits for state elected officials, Cuomo could, Moses-like, persist for an indefinite amount of time.

Like Moses, Cuomo was fond of artificial set pieces—strolling through subway tunnels and staging press conferences on bridges—that reporters typically devoured, helping to project the image of a get-it-done governor. Cuomo managed to always win, in the sense that his reputation suffered no serious damage for his stream of missteps, corruption, and outright failure. Each time, it seemed like a reckoning would come. But it never did.

TALLY

In the late spring, coronavirus cases had fallen enough that New York City could begin to reopen. On May 31, Cuomo announced a new low for daily statewide deaths: 56. Hospital and ICU admissions were on the decline. For more than two months, the largest city in America had been under the most intensive lockdown it had ever known. New York PAUSE had successfully, in the new parlance, flattened the curve. Cuomo and de Blasio were, for once, in lockstep. If tens of thousands of people hadn't already died, the celebration of America's governor could have had serious merit.

Other regions north of the city, where the virus had not yet infected as many, were able to inch ahead first. Cuomo had devised a four-phase reopening plan for the state: manufacturing, construction, and retail could open first, followed by malls, gyms, and indoor dining—though city residents wouldn't be able to dine indoors, at limited capacity, until September. The last phase included education, both K-12 and higher education, professional sports with no fans, and "low-risk" outdoor arts and entertainment. In the summer, the Toronto Blue Jays came to play their abbreviated 60-game season at Sahlen Field in Buffalo, the home of the Buffalo Bisons, a minor league team. Canada, its border closed to America, would not permit the Blue Jays to travel into and out of the country.

First, Cuomo had unveiled his coronavirus mountain. A second flourish came in July: the "New York Tough" poster. For the reporters who followed Cuomo, it was less of a surprise—the governor had a long-running affinity for the cartoonish melodrama of late 19th- and early 20th-century campaign posters. But for the general public, it was a curious reveal, one more example of Cuomo's instinctual self-aggrandizement reaching a wider audience.

The poster depicted a mountain, once more, to represent coronavirus deaths. A quote, from Cuomo himself, ran across the top: "Wake Up America! Forget the Politics, Get Smart!" Elsewhere, an octopus guided a cruise ship, Donald Trump sat on a crescent moon (labeled "it's only the flu"), and a vaguely Asiatic dragon blew the "Winds of Fear." There were inside jokes like Boyfriend Cliff, a nod to the mocked partner of one of Cuomo's daughters. Off to the right, an airplane labeled "Europeans" and "Jan–Mar" flew toward the mountain, symbolizing Cuomo's long-running contention that Trump's late decision to bar travelers from Europe was the primary reason so many died in New York.

"What we did was historic because we did tame the beast," Cuomo said on July 13 as he introduced the garish poster. "We did turn the corner. We did plateau that mountain. And then we came down the other side."

The poster, now on sale for $11.50, had its detractors. "I mean this with 0% snark: how is this not wildly offensive?" asked one Democratic state senator on Twitter. "This is an artful monument to death and tragedy being sold by the state. I'm legit perplexed."[104]

At the time of his poster unveiling, more than 32,000 New Yorkers had died statewide of coronavirus, a death toll far beyond any found in any state in America. The initial outbreak had not been contained. The amount of cold bodies tossed into morgues was difficult to fathom. But for Cuomo, such realities were not worth dwelling on. He wasn't sorry and he wasn't humbled.

In his narrative of triumph, there were two theses, repeated for the benefit of a sympathetic press corps, that explained the carnage away.

One, studies had shown the coronavirus in New York traced its origins to Europe. Since Trump didn't ban travel from Europe until 11:59 p.m. on March 13, Cuomo argued in his many press conferences and memoir that an earlier travel ban, like the one leveled against China in the beginning of February, could have spared New York. Cuomo would even go as far to label coronavirus the "European virus," a bid to counter Trump's "China virus" sloganeering.

"We acted two months after the China outbreak. When you look back, does anyone think the virus was still in China waiting for us to act two months later?" Cuomo said. "The horse had already left the barn by the time we moved."[105]

What Cuomo neglected to mention was that San Francisco, a city that theoretically benefited from Trump's China travel ban, already had as many as 9,700 undetected cases by the start of March, according to the Northeastern University study, a higher per capita rate than New York City's. Seattle had more than 2,000 cases. Most public health experts understood, by early March, closing down the city as much as possible and enforcing social distancing would slow the spread of the virus.

A belated European travel ban could not explain why Cuomo waited until March 22 to implement a shelter-in-place order and explicitly barred de Blasio from doing so days earlier. It did not explain why he dithered on a statewide shutdown of schools, unlike governors elsewhere.

It did not explain why a Democratic governor could repeatedly compare COVID-19 to the flu and tell rightfully terrified constituents that fear was worse than the virus itself.

Cuomo introduced another pernicious falsehood, mimicked by Republicans elsewhere, that he used to explain his own inability to prevent mass death in New York: it was density's fault.

"Why New York? Why are we seeing this level of infection? Well, why cities across the country? It's very simple. It's about density," Cuomo said in mid-April, when New York had already recorded more than 10,000 deaths, most of them in the city. "It's about the number of people in a small geographic location allowing that virus to spread and that virus is very good at what it does, it is a killer, it is very good at spreading, it is very contagious and dense environments are its feeding grounds."

Cuomo, accompanied by slides titled "Density" and "Exposure in dense environments," went on to add that rural counties could spread the virus, too, if enough people were packed together. But the nuance tacked on was lost in the primary message, which had been first popularized in March when he tweeted that there is a "density level in NYC that is destructive."[106] For casual observers, the reasoning was obvious: New York City, a very crowded place in which people live closely together, allowed coronavirus to spread, and this was why it was hit so much harder than elsewhere.

The argument arose from a parochial anti-urbanism that had little evidence to undergird it. San Francisco was America's second densest city. By the end of 2020, 176 people had died of coronavirus there. New York City, even after driving cases far down from their tragic peak, had 142 times as many deaths, though it was not nearly 142 times as dense. Denser cities across the world, including Seoul and Tokyo, experienced far lower death tolls. Decisions made by governments, local and national, made the biggest difference—not how close people happened to be packed together.

Cuomo appeared to be conflating density with *crowding*, no small difference when communicating with millions of people daily. Density is the number of people per square mile of land. Crowding is when a large group of people convene together in a small place.

"The reason Cuomo is putting his eggs in the density basket is because, unlike crowding, he can't control density and therefore he can't be blamed for the outcome," argued the urbanist Aaron Carr. "But knowing that he could control crowding early, and didn't, the question then becomes, 'why did Cuomo delay?,' and that is the last question Cuomo wants to answer."[107]

Soon enough, none of this would be theoretical anymore. Coronavirus eventually reached areas of the country far less dense than New York City, causing enormous suffering. North Dakota, a state with only 762,000 residents stretched over more than 70,000 square miles, would have the fourth-highest death rate in America. Other rural counties in Texas, South Dakota, and Iowa were pummeled too.

The density distraction hampered and stigmatized New York City in the early months of the pandemic. Residents fled the subway, believing it to be a vector for coronavirus, and tourists shied away. Housing prices boomed in the suburbs. The city's recovery would depend, in part, on convincing would-be New Yorkers that the city was a safe place to live. The Dakotas, even after enduring some of the worst viral outbreaks in America, wouldn't ever be viewed as hotbeds for future transmissions.

Cuomo eventually abandoned discussions of density, especially as coronavirus cases plummeted in the summer and other matters seized the popular consciousness. In late May, George Floyd, an unarmed Black man, was killed by Minneapolis police officers, igniting protests that rocked towns and cities across America. Though pandemic-related lockdown orders were still in effect, protesters flooded streets in the five boroughs, largely marching peacefully. There was unrest, however, and on one particular night, stores were looted and damaged in Manhattan and the Bronx.

On the afternoon of Monday, June 1, Governor Andrew Cuomo announced on an upstate radio show that New York City would have its first curfew since 1945.

"I know something has to be done," Cuomo said.

Though Cuomo couched the curfew announcement, in part, over concerns with the spread of COVID-19, its real purpose was to crack down on the isolated rioting that had taken place during the protests. "It's New York City, where I do believe there are people who use the chaos of the moment. It's an opportunity. If you want to steal, that's the night to do it. If you are an extremist group, and you want to preach anarchy, that's the night to do it," Cuomo said.[108]

Later in the day, de Blasio and Cuomo announced the curfew together in a news release. But New York City could do little without the approval of state government, thanks to Cuomo's executive order from March. Cuomo had the power to override a curfew imposed by a locality or implement one without their approval.

Yet de Blasio, who publicly embraced the curfew, quickly became the face of this disastrous response. Rather than de-escalate the protests, the order merely encouraged police to kettle, assault, and arrest unarmed New Yorkers who were marching beyond a curfew that, at first, extended to 11:00 p.m. and then dropped to 8:00 p.m. Police violated the city's own executive order by mass arresting protesters without a warning to disperse.

The backlash was swift. De Blasio was deluged daily with calls for his resignation. A Republican city councilman even called on Cuomo to invoke his obscure but very real legal power to remove de Blasio from office. Hundreds of former de Blasio administration staffers gathered outside City Hall to denounce the man they once believed would be a force for progressive change in the city.

De Blasio's blithe and delusional defense of his police force—a report from the city's Department of Investigation would find that the NYPD "lacked a clearly defined strategy tailored to respond to the large-scale protests of police and policing" and the State Attorney General, in turn, would bring a lawsuit against the police department[109]—made him an easy scapegoat for the curfew.

The legitimate rage and the calls for de Blasio's resignation played perfectly into Cuomo's hands. De Blasio was the front man for a reviled policy. Cuomo, again, receded into the background, leaving a lame-duck mayor to absorb a week of horrendous local and national press. It was a maneuver Cuomo had perfected; take credit for successes that were barely his own and avert blame for failures that were directly his doing.

It remained unclear if the curfew had even been de Blasio's idea. The mayor enforced it with enthusiasm. He could have publicly repudiated Cuomo and chose not to. He could have challenged him.

Instead, he accepted reality on Cuomo's terms. It was the easiest decision to make.

★ ★ ★

For all his success with the media, Cuomo could not quite shake the nursing home issue. Enough time had passed to reveal it as more than just a partisan talking point. First, in July, the Democrat-controlled legislature met to force a repeal of the deeply unpopular immunity provision for nursing homes and hospitals. For months, these institutions had been shielded from virtually all lawsuits, even those unrelated to coronavirus.

Progressive Democrats in the legislature hoped for a full, retroactive repeal: those impacted from the end of March onward would be able to sue. But Cuomo, in concert with hospital and nursing home lobbyists, would not allow that. Legislative leaders deferred to Cuomo. A state senator co-sponsoring the repeal legislation—one who had been a critic of the governor—had the bill yanked from her and handed off to a different senator. Retroactive immunity was taken off the table. More importantly, when the bill was finalized and sent to Cuomo's desk in late July, immunity related to coronavirus cases was left intact. The definition of the bill had simply been narrowed: nursing homes and hospitals would no longer have immunity for care not related to COVID-19. In early August, Cuomo signed the bill into law.

Democrats in the legislature, if unwilling to challenge the heart of the immunity law, were growing increasingly restless—sidelined for much of the summer, they were hardly a factor in government any longer. As far as most New Yorkers knew, government was simply Andrew Cuomo.

At the beginning of August, lawmakers hoped to change that. They would, at least, convene hearings to examine how and why so many people had died in New York nursing homes. They would even seek to figure out what the true death toll was. Cuomo's health commissioner, Dr. Howard Zucker, was summoned to testify.

Cuomo had already launched an investigation of his own, but in the fashion of most fact-finding missions authorized by his state government, its independence was questionable. In April, Cuomo joined with Letitia James, a close ally and the state attorney general, to commence a joint investigation of the nursing home industry.

Would the investigation include a review of the state's actions—including Cuomo's order forcing nursing homes to admit COVID-19 patients? And how could the AG and the governor fairly investigate an agency that the governor controlled? These questions were never quite answered. Though the facilities were often privately run, it was the state Department of Health that licensed the 613 long-term care facilities, and set regulations for how they operate.

The inherent nature of the attorney general's office, no matter who held it, could preclude effective investigations of the executive branch, since it derived some of its power and most of its funding from the governor.

"It is very hard for an agency to investigate itself. It doesn't mean it's a matter of corruption. It's just a matter of a conflict of interest," explained Berit Berger, the executive director of the Center for the Advancement of Public Integrity at Columbia University. "Certainly by having the executive involved, it's opening it up for critics to say this isn't a fair investigation."[110]

State lawmakers had called for an outside, independent investigation, with at least some asking for a 9/11 Commission-like body to investigate the entirety of the state's failed response. That didn't materialize. Instead, they would settle for the hearings, held remotely instead of in the chambers of the New York State Capitol.

Zucker appeared on August 3. For the lawmakers present and those watching from home, at least one fact was made startling clear: Cuomo's government really had no idea how many people died in their nursing homes.

"You don't have a ballpark you can give? So the total official number is 6,500, so is the total deaths with hospitals included 8,000, 10,000, 15,000?" asked James Skoufis, a Democratic state senator.

"I am not prepared to give you a specific number," Zucker responded.[111]

Outside public health experts estimated the nursing home death toll could be far higher than the reported deaths, which had numbered more than 6,400 by then. Some estimated New York could have undercounted deaths by many thousands. There was simply no way to know. State Health Department surveys showed in August that 21,000 nursing home beds were lying empty, 13,000 more than expected. It was an increase of almost double the official state nursing home death tally. While some of that increase could be attributed to fewer new admissions and people pulling residents out, it suggested that many others who aren't there anymore had died.[112]

The Empire Center, a right-leaning think tank active in analyzing the fiscal and legislative affairs of New York, sued Cuomo's Department of Health after the agency refused to release records showing the full count of coronavirus deaths among nursing home residents, including those that occurred after patients were sent to hospitals.

On the basis of this faulty data, though, the Cuomo administration attempted to exonerate itself. In July, the Department of Health released a report, aided by the consulting firm McKinsey & Company, that determined the state wasn't to blame for the nursing home deaths. The July report declared that the controversial March directive—which forced nursing homes to readmit coronavirus patients—had nothing to do with the spread of coronavirus and instead blamed staff working in the homes for unwittingly transmitting it to residents.

The report's data showed that nursing home deaths peaked a week before readmissions of patients who had tested positive for COVID-19 peaked. The height of infections of staff similarly tracked with peak mortality for residents, according to the report, with deaths peaking on April 8. Because the time from infection to death ranged between 18 and 25 days, the report argued that residents were likely infected by staff in mid-March, before the March 25 directive that forced nursing homes to readmit coronavirus patients.

Outside healthcare analysts, scientists, and epidemiologists overwhelmingly assailed the report for its faulty methodology. The report proclaimed that 80 percent of nursing homes that accepted coronavirus patients already had confirmed cases before the March 25 order, but didn't address the other 20 percent. The question state lawmakers were seeking to answer was, did readmitted residents spread coronavirus there? The Cuomo administration repeatedly refused to say.

If infected residents who were transferred to hospitals to die were excluded, how could the Department of Health definitively know that peak mortality came on April 8?

"If you're not counting those people, you're not seeing the whole picture," said Bill Hammond, the director of health policy at the Empire Center. "It's shocking to me, in context of what's supposed to be a scientific fact-based analysis, that the report continues to lowball the number of deaths."

The hearings drew critical media coverage, but closure didn't come then. It was only in January 2021, with a report from the state attorney general's office, that a fuller picture of the carnage came into focus: the state had undercounted nursing home deaths by as much as 50 percent. On the day of the report's release, on January 28, New York State had recorded, officially, 8,711 nursing home deaths. Hours after the report was made public, the Cuomo administration revised their tally: 12,743, an increase of 46 percent.[113]

Not long after, in response to the AG report and a lawsuit from the Empire Center, the Cuomo administration was forced to revise the nursing home death toll even higher. Another 1,516 deaths were added in just one February weekend. In total, the nursing home death tally had increased by an astounding 63 percent in just 10 days.[114]

"Some facilities reported the location of the person at the time of death inconsistently," the report said, making it difficult to determine whether the person who died was considered a patient of a nursing home or hospital. "A significantly higher number of resident COVID-19 deaths can be identified than is reflected in deaths publicized by DOH [the State Department of Health]."

Lawmakers, incensed, trained their fire directly at the governor.

"Governor Cuomo and the New York State Department of Health treated our elders as expendable, as if their lives were nothing more than the cost of doing business," said Biaggi, the Bronx Democratic state senator.

Cuomo was not chastened. Like other powerful politicians well-practiced in the art of self-defense and aggrievement, he would not apologize. To apologize was to admit weakness and fault. The Queens native in the White House could never say he was sorry, no matter how egregious the offense. The Queens native in the governor's mansion wasn't about to, either.

"If you look at New York State, we have a lower percentage of deaths in nursing homes than other states," Cuomo said at a press conference the day after the report was released. "A third of all deaths in this nation are from nursing homes."

Cuomo's argument was not wrong in a technical sense; it was merely misleading. The percentage of nursing home deaths was low, in part, because there had never been a proper tally. By citing the percentage, though, Cuomo was inadvertently making an argument against himself—the number was *also* relatively low because the overall coronavirus death toll, now beyond 40,000, was so extraordinarily high.

"New York State, we're only about 28 percent—only—but we're below the national average in number of deaths in nursing homes," Cuomo continued. "But who cares—33, 29—died in the hospital, died in a nursing home? They died."

For Cuomo, the usual approach could not keep working. A pliant national media and political class were not going to furnish his myth any longer. He could not bulldoze past facts and deride the critics who brought them to him. In February, his top aide, Melissa DeRosa, privately admitted to Democratic lawmakers the state had intentionally withheld the true nursing home death toll. She said the Cuomo administration was worried about a Department of Justice investigation. DeRosa argued Trump could start tweeting that "we killed everyone in nursing homes."

"Basically, we froze," she said in recorded remarks that were leaked to the *New York Post*.[115]

The revelation marked a profound, and perhaps lasting, turning point in Cuomo's relationship with the politicians in his own party. For months, it was Republicans, along with a vocal minority of progressive Democrats, assailing Cuomo over his handling of the pandemic. But now more Democrats were willing to move against him, with many state legislators calling for the revocation of the sweeping emergency powers he had won from the legislature almost a year earlier. (They eventually would.)

DeRosa's story, with time, seemed to crumble as well. The *New York Times* later reported that Cuomo's aides had rewritten a report with a higher nursing home death tally before DeRosa ever interacted with Trump's Department of Justice. The numbers were suppressed just as Cuomo was beginning work on his triumphant memoir.

In February 2021, Ron Kim, the state assemblyman who had clashed with Cuomo over his handling of nursing homes, told multiple media outlets that the governor had called him up personally and threatened to "destroy" his political career. "It was a 10-minute, one-sided, screaming and yelling, where I felt threatened, that if I didn't act in a certain way, to issue a statement, not tomorrow, tonight in his own words, that there would be retribution against me," Kim recalled.[116]

What made the episode remarkable was its fallout: for one of the very first times in Cuomo's decade-long reign, another politician got the best of him in the media. Kim was a mainstay of the major cable TV networks and newspapers, his story relayed repeatedly. Cuomo was roundly denounced. Kim became, for a moment at least, the most famous state legislator in America. On

February 19, he appeared on *The View,* one of the nation's most popular talk shows, where he called Cuomo an "abuser."

Privately, Cuomo was fuming. He could not stop Kim from talking. He could not crush him, as he had so many old adversaries. Not only had his threats proved ineffective, they had backfired utterly, revealing to the public the petty vindictiveness those in politics had long known. Unhinged threats across a telephone line represented twentieth century political warfare; Kim and the young progressives in Albany belonged to the new century, nimble enough to challenge Cuomo's power directly.

Quickly, another bombshell arrived: it was reported in February that the U.S. attorney in Brooklyn and the FBI had launched a preliminary investigation into the Cuomo administration's handling of nursing home data. Possible avenues of interest included false statements and any scheme to defraud the federal government of funds. A spokesman for Cuomo said they would cooperate with the probe.

Just a week later, Lindsey Boylan, a political candidate and former Cuomo aide, would make the first allegation of sexual harassment against the governor. The scandals would converge, and soon dozens of Democratic politicians, including both of New York's senators, would be calling for Cuomo to resign.

★ ★ ★

When Bill de Blasio, who was still the mayor theoretically in charge of New York City's school system, suggested in April

2020 that the public schools, shuttered for nearly a month, would remain closed through the end of the current school year, Andrew Cuomo shrugged him off like he was little more than a second-rate newspaper columnist.

"That's his opinion. He didn't close them and he can't open them," Cuomo said. "It happened on a metropolitan-wide basis and we'll act on a metropolitan basis, coordinating with Nassau, Suffolk and Westchester."

Cuomo was right. *He* decided whether New York City's public school system, serving a million children, opened or closed. His executive order, issued to blunt de Blasio's attempt to lock down the city as coronavirus was infecting and killing thousands, made it only more so. Closing the schools, for the de Blasio administration, had been a fraught endeavor because there was little preparation for remote learning and because so many students, particularly those from poor families, relied on the buildings for meals and afterschool programs.

Cuomo was glad, after finally forcing de Blasio's hand in March, to make him the public face of such a challenging issue. Just as with the citywide curfew, de Blasio would prove a useful figurehead for Cuomo, designated to absorb the wrath of every conceivable interest group.

Like elsewhere in the country, remote learning could not replicate the in-person class experience in New York. Students struggled to learn the same way behind a laptop or tablet screen as they would sitting across from a teacher. They missed their friends. Some did not have reliable internet connections at all.

The city's 111,600 homeless students were the worst off, dispersed among shelters and shared housing arrangements. For students with significant cognitive and emotional challenges, remote learning posed a particular, unresolvable challenge. These students needed to be physically near their instructors, in a school building. When schools first shut down in March, teachers were given just three days in person to begin mapping out how to transition their curriculum digitally.

Schools, of course, would stay shut through June, and Cuomo knew this. He was likely smarting from de Blasio's decision to simply text him, at the last minute, before making the decision public. It was rare payback from City Hall after years of Cuomo doing the same. But de Blasio should have understood he was not operating by the old rules any longer—this was the pandemic, and Cuomo was king.

New York City's school system is singular in the state, and not only because of its size and diversity. Unlike other localities, there is no traditional school board with elected members. Instead, control of the schools—the Department of Education—is centralized under the aegis of the mayor in a system known as mayoral control. Mayoral control debuted under Michael Bloomberg, who fought to dissolve the old local school boards, which exercised great sway over neighborhood schools and made it difficult for any one mayor to make sweeping policy change. Most educators, in the long run, judged mayoral control a success because it eliminated inefficiencies and certain neighborhood fiefdoms. The mayor, instead of the school board, could select the leader of the citywide school system. Accountability rested with City Hall.

New York City, on its own, could not simply decide to do this. Bloomberg needed the approval of the governor and the state legislature. Since Bloomberg was both a billionaire and a Republican, and the governor of New York was a Republican and his party controlled the State Senate in the early 2000s, gaining full control of city schools was plausible. Mayoral control was granted a seven-year trial period and renewed again in 2009 for another six years.

In 2015, de Blasio, then in his second year as mayor, went to Albany to ask to make the extension permanent. Republicans and Democrats alike, including Cuomo, rebuffed him. Public education was one area of many in which Cuomo and de Blasio, though both Democrats, did not find much agreement.

De Blasio, like most left-leaning Democrats in the city, was a supporter of traditional public schools and closely aligned with teachers unions. He believed in funneling more money into schools and providing so-called wraparound services, like afterschool programs, so they could function like community centers.

Cuomo was a vigorous supporter of charter schools and, in his first term at least, openly disdained the teachers unions. Publicly-funded but privately-operated, charter schools exploded under Bloomberg, and were a favorite of both conservative Republicans and Democrats who wanted more standardized testing and aggressive oversight of teachers. Many of Cuomo's top donors, including the hedge fund billionaire Daniel Loeb, were charter schools enthusiasts because they could operate without a unionized workforce. Successful charter schools retained support from some neighborhoods where they offered alternatives to less popular public schools.

Cuomo's education legacy was forged early. In 2014, de Blasio was attempting to gain support for an income tax hike to fund his universal prekindergarten program. New York City couldn't raise income taxes without the approval of Cuomo and the state legislature.

Cuomo had spent his first term attempting to shrink the scope of government and decrease taxes on the wealthy. Though de Blasio had won his mayoral race on this promise, Cuomo was adamant that taxes would not be raised on anyone. De Blasio persisted. Cuomo eventually counteroffered: instead of a dedicated, renewable tax stream, the state would just promise to fund the program for several years. De Blasio, still believing he had political capital, pushed harder for a tax increase. He got nowhere.

The program would be funded. But Cuomo got his revenge. As winter turned to spring, he met with charter school advocates and told them to organize a large rally in Albany. They complied, staging one on the same day de Blasio rallied for his pre-K program.

Cuomo joined the charter school masses. "You are not alone," he told the thundering crowd. "We will save charter schools."

In the state budget passed soon after, Cuomo had a surprise for de Blasio: charter schools now had the most expansive protections in America. New York City would either have to find free space for all charter schools in public school buildings or pay their rent elsewhere. No other school district anywhere had such a requirement.

Public spending on charter school rent accelerated greatly after the law took effect in 2014.[117] Rising from $33.2 million in the first year, New York City eventually spent more than $100 million annually on paying the rent bills for charter schools. The Department of Education even ended up paying the rent for a handful of charter schools whose foundations or LLCs outright own their buildings.

Cuomo's embrace of charters and undercutting of teachers unions was enough for him to fail to win the endorsement of the New York State United Teachers, the statewide union, when he ran for reelection in 2014. Cuomo's opponent was a conservative Republican, but the union backed no one. "Those who earn endorsements are friends of public education and labor," said Karen Magee, NYSUT's president at the time. "Over the last two years, they earned our support by advocating effectively for our public schools, colleges and healthcare institutions; listening intently to the concerns and aspirations of our members, and voting consistently the right way."[118]

Cuomo couldn't win their support in 2018 either, but the unions had grown less resistant to him by virtue of his persistence. He was the governor, after all, and he wasn't going anywhere. And he had stopped openly advocating for charter schools as Democrats gained power in the state legislature, making such a political fight less appetizing.

The United Federation of Teachers, the union representing all New York City schoolteachers, was one of the most influential in the state and their president, Michael Mulgrew, had become a Cuomo ally. Both were from the outer boroughs of New York—Mulgrew was a Staten Island native—and neither had much affection for the progressive Democrats rising in the state. Mulgrew had been tacitly supportive of Cuomo's decision to help create an alliance between rogue Democrats and Republicans that maintained a GOP majority in the State Senate.

De Blasio had his own working relationship with Mulgrew, though it appeared to grow chillier as Cuomo drew closer to the union power broker. As the new school year approached in September, the pandemic lingering, de Blasio began to argue that schools needed to reopen in-person.

The debate's usual left–right axis had been scrambled. In July, as coronavirus cases waned in certain parts of the country, including New York, Trump declared "SCHOOLS MUST OPEN IN THE FALL!!!" Trump was no deep thinker on education; he simply worried shuttered schools could hurt the economy and endanger his reelection chances. But he had inadvertently aligned himself with some education experts who believed remote learning was doing great damage to schoolchildren. Trump's support for reopening, however, all but doomed the project with many liberals, including teachers who believed he was sacrificing their health for his own political fortunes.

In New York City, the reopening saga was peculiar. De Blasio was treated, once more, as the politician who would dictate the future of the schools. The media fixated on him; interest groups, at varying points, gathered against him. But it was Cuomo who would have to sign off on any declaration or decree. It was Cuomo's school system. At best, de Blasio was a junior partner, offering recommendations to the executive suite.

In August, Cuomo batted down de Blasio's first attempt at a reopening plan, citing a lack of specifics. "The concepts are not enough. Where is the personnel? Where is the equipment? How are you going to do this?" Cuomo asked, granting a 14-day extension for the city to submit another plan. Days later, Cuomo decreed that all schools statewide could open in the fall if they wanted to. Otherwise, he left the details up to individual school districts. At any point, he could scuttle de Blasio's plan, but he had no interest in offering his own.

Many questions remained, and de Blasio's leadership and communication style were halting at best, bewildering at worst. The mayor called for children to report to school one to three days a week and learn online the rest of the time, a plan that would present a challenge for many working parents. Rightful concerns cropped up about whether there were enough nurses to staff all city school buildings. Many buildings themselves were aging and some ventilation systems were in urgent need of upgrades. Rank-and-file teachers feared they would be on the frontlines of another viral outbreak.

It was not Cuomo's problem when Mulgrew's union, at the end of August, threatened a strike. De Blasio had set a September 10 start date and was sticking to it. Mulgrew said it was much too soon, given the safety challenges. If schools opened, Mulgrew warned in his own bridge-and-tunnel accent, "it might be one of the biggest debacles in the history of the city."[119] The city's principals' union, citing the poor ventilation systems and a lack of availability of personal protective equipment and cleaning supplies, backed the UFT. New York State law barred public employees from striking, but some in the union were willing to incur the stiff, daily fines to push back the reopening date.

The strike was averted after de Blasio and Mulgrew agreed to delay the start of schools to September 21, though there were still rank-and-file teachers upset with returning physically. Transitional days were added for remote and hybrid—a mix of remote and in-person—learning. As part of the agreement, de Blasio resented that schools would close if the positivity rate for coronavirus in New York City rose above 3 percent. At the time, positive rates were hovering under 1 percent, a remarkable decrease from the spring.

Three percent, for Cuomo, was just too high. "A 3 percent infection rate, you know, that's a high infection rate in a congregate situation. Three percent is high in a dense environment, like a dense urban environment where you have people taking public transportation; it's a crowded environment," he said. "Three percent is high."

It was lower, though, than his own standard set for the rest of the state: 9 percent for K-12 schools.

The beginning of the school year would be unlike any other. Only about a quarter of the city's students attended in-person instruction. More than 500,000 students sat at home, taking online classes. Still, New York was the rare major school system nationwide offering in-person learning at all. Los Angeles and Chicago had begun the year fully remote. For the teachers and students that remained in public school buildings, the threat of infection turned out to be more marginal than feared. Among those tested by the end of October, the positive rate was an extremely low .15 percent.[120]

Beyond the walls of the school, however, coronavirus was creeping back. In October, Cuomo published his memoir, *American Crisis*, which briefly reached the *New York Times'* bestseller list. Not long after, as public health experts predicted, cases began rising again as winter approached. Damaging outbreaks were now north of the city, in rural counties of the state and in smaller cities that had been spared the brunt of the first wave, like Buffalo. Hospitalizations spiked anew. New York City had likely been hit too hard already to suffer an exact repeat of the spring—more than 25,000 dead, a positivity rate exceeding 30 percent—but more could still get sick and die.

Overriding de Blasio, Cuomo had developed his own color-coded system to highlight infections and order closures of schools and businesses. Rolled out in October, as micro-clusters of cases began cropping up in parts of the city and suburban counties, the system divided localities into three zones: red, orange, and yellow. Red zones, which banned all mass gatherings, shut schools, and cut down the capacity on houses of worship to 25 percent, covered Orthodox Jewish neighborhoods where coronavirus cases were spiking. At one of his press briefings, Cuomo had used a 14-year-old photo of a Hasidic funeral to warn against mass gatherings, outraging many Orthodox leaders and publications.

"WILL CUOMO APOLOGIZE?!?" cried a headline in *The Yeshiva World* newspaper.[121]

It was a strange position for Cuomo, a foreign policy hawk who had made several high-profile trips to Israel during his tenure, to find himself in—a target of ire for religious Jews. As coronavirus restrictions tightened in Borough Park, an Orthodox Jewish neighborhood in Brooklyn, protesters poured into the streets, burning face masks in the middle of the road. A mob swarmed a photographer and beat a Hasidic man, accusing him of disloyalty to the community. An Orthodox Jewish journalist who had been reporting on the pandemic was hit in the head and kicked by the crowd.

Their rage, though, was most targeted at Cuomo. Three Jewish congregations in the suburb of Rockland County sued him, claiming he engaged in a "streak of anti-Semitic discrimination." The merits of the lawsuit were unclear, but reflected a hardened belief, among Orthodox Jews at least, that Cuomo now hated them. In early October, four Orthodox elected officials in

Brooklyn released a joint statement accusing Cuomo of pursuing a "scientifically and constitutionally questionable shutdown of our communities" and having an "utter lack of coordination and communication with local officials."[122]

If Cuomo had failed to adequately communicate the new restrictions before they went into effect—a contention shared among just about every Orthodox leader—he wasn't going to admit it now. Asked several weeks later if he'd apologize to the Orthodox Jewish community, as de Blasio had recently done, Cuomo was blunt: "No."

"I am sorry that they feel the disruption, I am sorry that they are disrupted, their religious ceremonies are disrupted," he continued, "how many people they can have in a synagogue is disrupted, how many people they can have at a wedding is disrupted, the operation of their schools is disrupted. I am sorry for that."

★ ★ ★

In November, Joe Biden defeated Donald Trump. New Yorkers cheered wildly from stoops and street corners, streaming into parks, bars, and a once desolate Times Square to celebrate what had felt like, to many, the end of a long war. For the afternoon and evening, there would be no warnings from politicians about coming together, sometimes without masks, to hug, kiss, dance, and drink.

The virus, though, did not care about current events. Cases continued to rise in the five boroughs, ticking up each week. Every metric—positivity, hospitalizations—was trending in a dangerous direction. Cuomo, this time, would permit de Blasio to make a difficult and misguided decision.

As the city's positive rate steadily neared 3 percent, the mayor announced in November he would be shutting schools once more. De Blasio called it a "temporary" situation. But Cuomo, as always, possessed the ultimate authority. Earlier in the day, at a November 19 press briefing, Cuomo was pressed on the status of city schools.

One journalist, the *Wall Street Journal*'s Albany reporter, asked Cuomo directly if city schools would stay open, adding that there was confusion over whether city officials or the governor had the authority to close schools after Cuomo said the area could be declared an orange zone and schools would subsequently shut down.

"What are you talking about?" Cuomo snapped back. "Follow the facts!"

The reporter explained that he was confused by the facts, noting that many New York City parents were also failing to understand the governor's plan.

"I'll tell you what, Jimmy. They're not confused. You're confused," Cuomo groused, referring to the reporter, Jimmy Vielkind. "Read the law and you won't be confused."

Another reporter backed Vielkind up.

"I don't really care what you think. Of course, you agree with him, because you're in the same business with him," Cuomo said.[123]

City schools, about an hour later, shuttered, with de Blasio making the announcement. This time, parents mobilized against de Blasio, angry that their children were denied in-person learning when so few coronavirus cases had been found in schools. Several protested outside Gracie Mansion, the mayor's residence.

A few weeks later, the public schools did reopen—partially, at least. Pre-K and elementary school students returned to buildings, as well as students with disabilities. Middle and high school students wouldn't go back to classrooms until 2021, de Blasio said.

Unrelated to schools, coronavirus cases kept rising across the state, mirroring national trends. America was deep into a third wave, and newly rolled out vaccines wouldn't be widely available enough to keep more people from dying. More than 37,000 had died in New York already. Nationally, the death toll had surpassed 300,000, as the virus reached every region of the country.

Cuomo, in his news conference, had grown testier, wielding the right-wing rhetoric of personal responsibility to shame New Yorkers for the rising rate of cases. Surely, it couldn't be government's fault.

Not catching coronavirus, the governor declared, wouldn't be so different than going on a diet.

"I just want to make it very simple," Cuomo said in the late fall. "If you socially distanced and you wore a mask, and you were smart, none of this would be a problem. It's all self-imposed. It's all self-imposed. If you didn't eat the cheesecake, you wouldn't have a weight problem."[124]

Cuomo's memoir, published on October 13, had arrived before another coronavirus wave engulfed his own state. By year's end, positivity rates in New York City were north of 7 percent, when they had been below 1 percent in the late summer. Hospitalizations were at levels not seen since May.

Cuomo, perhaps, would have to write another book.

AUSTERITY

By the time Andrew Mark Cuomo reached puberty, the American progressive movement appeared to be in terminal decline. In 1972, when Cuomo turned 15, Richard Nixon won 49 states, obliterating the candidate of the grassroots left, George McGovern. The next Democratic president, Jimmy Carter, would govern on the terms of the new neoliberalism, distancing himself from a New Deal consensus that had been a bedrock of American politics for 40 years. In New York City, where Cuomo was born and raised, the manufacturing base, which had been the fuel for a fervent and radical trade union movement, had collapsed. Socialists disappeared from city life.

Three years after Nixon's victory, the richest and most famous city in America was hours from bankruptcy. Bankers no longer wanted to loan the big liberal city any money. A once-robust tax base was no more. Multiple mayors had strained the city's finances to save this safety net until, in the mid-1970s, they no longer could. Public schools, libraries, hospitals, afterschool programs, and garbage pick-up would be gutted so thoroughly that many would question the survival of the urban project itself, wondering if New York would simply hollow out from disinvestment and despair.

Among the smart men who would chart the future, there was a fresh consensus, one meant to supplant the liberalism of Franklin Roosevelt and Fiorello LaGuardia for all time. Government was just too *big*. Welfare rolls had to be slimmed or, ideally, vaporized altogether. Public universities could not just be free. Profligate spending, they said, had brought about a collapse that could only be rectified with smaller, wiser government, the titans of real estate and Wall Street preferably telling weak-willed Democratic politicians what to do.

Some, like the investment banker Felix Rohatyn, attempted to lend austerity a veneer of sagacity and even benevolence. Chairing the Municipal Assistance Corporation, Rohatyn had the final word on New York City's spending and taxes for nearly a decade, an unelected maven who decreed how much the public school teachers, firefighters, and sanitation workers would be paid.

Others were more insidious, if more direct. A leading light of urban affairs, Roger Starr, declared in 1976 that city government should abandon blighted areas like the South Bronx altogether, withdrawing police, public schools, and the basic municipal services that sustain an urban existence. Reinvestment, he said, was hopeless.

"The stretches of empty blocks may then be knocked down, services can be stopped, subway stations closed, and the land left to lie fallow until a change in economic and demographic assumptions makes the land useful once again," Starr wrote in the *New York Times* that year. "Better a thriving city of five million than a Calcutta of seven, destroyed by its internal wrangling."[125]

This was the city of Andrew Cuomo's youth, though he was sheltered from its darkest edges. Though he played up his working-class upbringing in his memoirs and interviews—behold, the beach-muscled, Italian outer-borough boy—his father was already on the way to being someone very important by the time he was old enough to do algebra and operate a motor vehicle. Andrew was Mario Cuomo's oldest son—it was Mario, the son of Italian immigrants, who could lay claim to the rags-to-richest origin tale, a tough kid from South Jamaica, Queens who put himself through law school and briefly played minor league baseball. Conceiving of himself as a "middle-class guy" in his memoir, Andrew wrote that he paid his own way through "school with every odd job imaginable: landscaper, night-shift security guard, mechanic, ice scream scooper, tow truck driver, and construction worker."[126] All true, though this obscures the fact that it was more a fatherly expectation of self-reliance than any kind of financial necessity that led to these odd jobs. By the time his son was towing trucks, Mario Cuomo was already famous.

Mario's rise to fame began in the bucolic, very white Queens neighborhood of Forest Hills, where the liberal Republican mayor, John Lindsay, wanted to build a new public housing development. The idea was noble: integrate more working-class New Yorkers, predominately of color, into a middle class area known for its good public schools and lower crime rate. The locals revolted, decrying the proposed three 24-story towers. They threw rocks and torches at protests. They massed at City Hall. Jimmy Carter, campaigning for president that year, promised he would not force racial integration that would disrupt the "ethnic purity" of a neighborhood.

Lindsay, fearing further backlash, recruited Mario, a 40-year-old attorney well-regarded for mediating another housing dispute in Queens, to broker a compromise.

He did. The 840 apartments originally proposed were reduced to 432, with 40 percent of the units reserved for the elderly. The towers ended up being just 12 stories tall. The city also adjusted maximum income levels and transformed the project into New York's first cooperative public low-income housing, in which residents were shareholders. The buildings became majority white.

In the next mayoral election, Mario later recalled, "none of the candidates argued for integration or dispersal of ghetto residents in middle-class areas."

"The new and safer emphasis was on rehabilitating the ghettos," he continued. "The clock had been turned back nearly two decades, and many people felt that the impetus for this withdrawal had been provided by Forest Hills."[127]

The elder Cuomo's career, though, was on an upswing. He had been defeated in a 1974 campaign for lieutenant governor but was selected to be a top aide to the new governor, Hugh Carey. In 1977, Carey urged him to run for mayor of New York City. After deliberating, Cuomo entered the race late but ran vigorously, standing out as a liberal who was against the death penalty. He came in second, losing to Ed Koch, a death penalty supporter.

"Looking back, I believe my father's candidacy was doomed from the moment of his late entry," Andrew Cuomo reflected in his first memoir, *All Things Possible.* "It was his first real race, and his campaign was amateurish. No one was in charge."[128]

The loss, however, would only set him up for 1982, when he bested Koch in a race for governor. The popular narrative of Mario Cuomo's 12 years in power revolved around his proud liberalism at a time when the country, under Ronald Reagan, was racing rightward. This was partially true. Mario was a leading figure in the Democratic Party. It was oft-rumored that he would run for president. New Yorkers had an affinity for him that outstripped anything enjoyed by his son in the pre-pandemic era. At the 1984 Democratic National Convention, Mario delivered a stirring defense of American liberalism—"you ought to know that this nation is more a 'tale of two cities' than it is just a 'shining city on a hill'"—that remained one of the most famous speeches to come out of a political convention.

Andrew Cuomo, in this narrative, wanted to be everything his father wasn't: a politician who, without glamour, got things done. And it was true, as obituaries of Mario later noted, that he had left behind little in the way of a *tangible* legacy. There were few signature accomplishments—no great infrastructure project, social safety net expansion, or new university system. He mostly built prisons.

However, Andrew did learn one important thing from his father. Quietly, Mario was not a liberal beacon. He cut budgets, shrunk welfare programs, and constantly frustrated liberals who were supposed to be on his side.

"While Mario faced legitimate pressure to impose drastic cuts, major targets of those cuts were the constituencies with the least political power, like the developmentally disabled and emotionally disturbed," recalled a former Democratic state assemblyman, Dan Feldman, upon seeing the governor's very first budget, in 1983. "Nowhere to be found was the 'compassion' that seemed so central an element of his inaugural address. Mario gave great speeches. But as time went on, the disconnect between what he said and what he did became ever more apparent."[129]

Once in office, Mario fought for tax cuts and shrinking state spending. "Jobs should come first, not welfare," he said in one speech. "Welfare should be only a last resort."[130]

There were Democrats in New York who wanted government to do more, especially as Reagan assaulted progressives from the White House. But within the State Senate they were firmly entrenched in the minority. This was a peculiar New York story: though Reagan would be the last Republican to carry the state in a presidential election, Republicans would control the State Senate, with only a brief interruption, from the late 1960s until 2019.

Gerrymandering and geographical disparities—Republicans were stronger in the suburbs and some rural areas—as well as a more robust voter registration history explained some of it. But the GOP in New York could always count on Democrats to sabotage their own, usually moderates wary of liberals in New York City having too much influence.

Quietly, Mario Cuomo was one of those moderates. Though widely popular in the state, he failed to aggressively campaign for State Senate Democrats or raise money for them. He rarely used his own formidable war chest to help Democrats. In the last two weeks of his successful reelection campaign in 1990, Cuomo had more than $5 million left to spend, a tremendous sum at the time. His opposition was weak and splintered.

But none of Mario's campaign cash "went to the hard-pressed Democratic candidates for the State Senate, who are borrowing money for the final stages of their effort to win control of the upper house of the Legislature, a campaign in which they have been outspent by the State Senate Republican Campaign Committee by at least four to one," the *New York Times* reported.[131]

Ironically, it was the much-maligned 1990 campaign effort that had begun with greater hope for Democrats. Unlike 1986, when he was much more popular and won reelection in a historic landslide, Mario declared he was sick and tired of Republicans running the upper chamber in Albany. This time, he said, he would actually fight for the Democrats.

He was, however, predictably vague.

"Mr. Cuomo did not say specifically what he would do but recommended a theme—'Take a chance on Democrats for a change'—and finding good candidates to run on that theme," the *Times* reported in 1988.

In 1992, when Bill Clinton was poised to defeat George H. W. Bush in New York, Senate Democrats were optimistic they could ride Clinton's coattails to victory. Republicans, again outspending them and again benefitting from gerrymandered districts, prevailed. Cuomo, meanwhile was too "consumed with campaign work on behalf of the Clinton-Gore ticket" and "had little time for specific campaigning for Democratic Senate candidates."[132]

Andrew played a very direct role in his father's administration. He was his father's first campaign manager, trusted enforcer, and sometime roommate. When Mario sought a fourth term in 1994 against a little-known Republican, George Pataki, Andrew was working in Washington, serving as the assistant secretary of the Department of Housing and Urban Development. (He would be the secretary just a few years later.)

Pataki, riding a national Republican wave, defeated Mario, whose campaign Andrew described as a "slow-motion automobile crash."[133]

"If you had run the campaign, I would have won," Andrew recalled his father telling him.

Andrew's humble opinion? "I believe that."[134]

Hungry for redemption, Andrew Cuomo returned to New York after a stint leading HUD under Bill Clinton. While serving Clinton, Cuomo fully embraced the president's neoliberal vision of governance. Adapting much of the Reagan agenda,

Clinton slashed welfare rolls, deregulated Wall Street, and pursued disruptive free trade. "Clinton had wisely taken the best of Republican principles—the private sector, not government, creates jobs and wealth—and combined it with the Democrats' philosophy: you can't pull yourself up by your bootstraps when you are stuck in the mud," Cuomo wrote.[135]

Cuomo's first campaign for governor, in 2002, was a failure. He challenged a popular politician, Carl McCall, in the Democratic primary. The state comptroller, McCall was vying to be New York's first Black governor. Cuomo campaigned as a political outsider, promising to slash taxes and reform Albany.

Pataki was still governor and his approval ratings, like Cuomo's 18 years later, had soared after a crisis—the September 11 attacks. In a gaffe that was tame by today's standards, Cuomo claimed during the campaign that Giuliani, and not Pataki, was the true leader after 9/11. "There was one leader for 9/11: it was Rudy Giuliani," Cuomo said aboard a campaign bus. "If it defined George Pataki, it defined George Pataki as not being the leader … He held the leader's coat. He was a great assistant to the leader. But he was not a leader."

Cuomo, facing both a media backlash from the Pataki comment and the realization that he could not beat McCall, dropped out just days before the primary. Clinton was at his side. In the moment, Cuomo believed his political career could be over. But it was revived in 2006, when he won an open Democratic primary for state attorney general and defeated the future Fox host, Jeanine Pirro.

Cuomo would have likely spent many years as the state's attorney general if not for Eliot Spitzer. A pugilistic liberal who had risen to prominence prosecuting Wall Street as attorney general, Spitzer was easily elected governor in 2006. Early in his first term, he was forced to resign in the midst of a prostitution scandal. Spitzer had been Cuomo's most formidable rival in state government and his weaker successor, David Paterson, struggled to finish the term. Cuomo pressured Paterson to not seek election in 2010 and became, by default, the governor-in-waiting.

There was no 2010 Democratic primary. Cuomo had the nomination by acclimation and breezed to victory against an incendiary Buffalo businessman, Carl Paladino.

Cuomo's first campaign for governor reflected his fundamental political beliefs. Unlike his father, he had no interest in speaking the language of the left. He campaigned, and would subsequently govern, as a triangulating Democrat, vowing to slash taxes, shrink government, and empower the state's finance and real estate lobbies against organized labor.

"We've seen the same play run for 10 years," Cuomo said shortly before his election. "The governor announces the budget, unions come together, put $10 million in a bank account, run television ads against the governor. The governor's popularity drops; the governor's knees weaken; the governor falls to one knee, collapses, makes a deal."[136]

The first term offered opportunities for an austerity governor. His predecessor, Paterson, had hiked taxes on millionaires to raise revenue as the state reeled from the 2008 economic crash. Cuomo strongly opposed maintaining the taxes, though relented after the Occupy Wall Street movement took off. He moved immediately, however, to slash Medicaid spending. Property taxes were capped, pleasing wealthier suburban voters but imperiling the public school districts that relied on the revenue.

Cuomo refused to comply with a long-running lawsuit that required New York State to more fairly fund poorer school districts. The public university system saw tuition increases and steadily reduced state spending. When the new mayor, Bill de Blasio, called for a minimum wage increase in New York City, Cuomo quickly rejected the idea. "We don't want to cannibalize ourselves," he said.[137]

If Cuomo swung left, it was on issues like same-sex marriage, which he legalized to much fanfare in 2011. He allowed Republicans, then in control of the State Senate, to gerrymander their own district lines a year later, cementing their majority for much of the 2010s. Progressives who wanted to further raise taxes on millionaires, codify Roe v. Wade in the state constitution, or protect rent-stabilized apartments in New York City would run into a wall of Republican opposition. For Cuomo, that was the reality he preferred.

It helped, too, that the Republicans would never support any kind of campaign finance reform. New York had some of the laxest laws in the nation, with donors able to form unlimited LLCs to circumvent restrictions. Millionaires and billionaires, as well as corporations, were allowed to donate more than $50,000 to Cuomo individually. These laws allowed Cuomo to swell his campaign war chest to levels undreamed of by most executives in America.

Twice Cuomo faced primaries from the left, from law professor Zephyr Teachout in 2014 and acclaimed actress and activist Cynthia Nixon in 2018, and each time—though he triumphed overwhelmingly—he had been forced to accept ever more liberal policy prescriptions. The Teachout campaign pressured him to ban fracking in New York. The legislative session following Nixon's campaign, with Democrats in full control of government, led to sweeping criminal justice reforms and stronger tenant and environmental protections.

★ ★ ★

Not long after Nixon kicked off her campaign against Cuomo, a man named Joe Percoco was found guilty in federal court of soliciting and accepting more than $300,000 in bribes. His photograph was in every major New York newspaper.

"Joe Percoco has played a lot of different roles in my life," Cuomo once explained. "He was my father's gubernatorial advance man in the 1990s, my special assistant at HUD, my campaign manager in 2002, my divorce counselor in 2003, and my fishing buddy on a Fourth of July fishing trip to the Hamptons."[138] More eloquently, perhaps, at Mario Cuomo's funeral, he referred to Percoco as "my father's third son, who sometimes I think he loved the most."

Mario's "third son" had seamlessly transitioned into an Andrew governorship. Officially he was the executive deputy secretary—more accurately, he was a direct extension of Andrew's cunning and wrath, calling up lawmakers, operatives, and lobbyists at all hours of the day and night to bully or cajole them into doing whatever it was Cuomo wanted in that particular moment. He was a hustler, a gatekeeper, a consigliere, a brother. "When you are getting close to the top of an issue, it's Joe Percoco you are sitting with," recalled one state senator.[139]

Now he was prison-bound. The corruption scandal, which revolved around a "low-show" job given to Percoco's wife by an energy company wanting to build a power plant in the Hudson Valley, exposed the Cuomo administration as everything it had promised not to be—venal, self-dealing, and suffused with cronyism and waste. The conviction came four years after Cuomo had shut down an anti-corruption commission of his own creation whose investigators began probing groups politically close to him.

Though they won a conviction of Percoco, federal prosecutors never reached Cuomo himself. But many political observers wondered how much the governor, a details-obsessed executive, knew about the corruption of his closest aide. It was evidence, at the very minimum, that something had gone very wrong in the executive branch.

Cuomo got his third term. His approval ratings, though, were slumping. Democrats in the legislature were no longer afraid of him. Progressives had made him embrace policy—a minimum wage hike, a fracking ban, protection of rent-stabilization—that never fit his ideological mold. He was gradually losing his ability to intimidate and overwhelm. Percoco's six-year prison sentence proved federal prosecutors were unafraid to target Cuomo's most innermost ring.

But the pandemic, in some sense, offered a restoration, a chance for Cuomo to return to what he had been. His popularity skyrocketed. The state of emergency—the executive orders he signed and the powers the legislature awarded to him—made him virtually the only person of significance in New York State.

The legislators who, just a year earlier, had been crowing about their victories over the governor were subordinated once more. After the passage of the state budget at the end March, the legislature didn't convene again for months.

With Percoco long gone, a new power broker had risen: Robert Mujica, the budget director. Mujica, like Cuomo, was a fiscal conservative. With the pandemic brutalizing New York's economy—once-thriving sectors like hospitality and tourism were wiped out overnight—tax revenue was suddenly scarce. Mujica was empowered to slash the budget throughout the year, thanks to the new powers Cuomo won during the budget negotiation process, but he decided, with no forewarning, to do something entirely different: he entirely *withheld* state money from towns, cities, and their public services indefinitely.

These were not, in the Orwellian contention of the Cuomo administration, budget cuts. They would function exactly as cuts would but could not be called cuts. If they were, the state legislature would be legally required to offer a counterproposal. The dark brilliance of redefining budget cuts this way—simply not delivering the money at all, and claiming it could come later—meant that Cuomo could truly govern alone.

At the end of April, Cuomo warned state spending could be slashed by as much as $10 billion. More than $8 billion in cuts would be reserved for "aid-to-localities," Albany-speak for the state money that propped up public schools, public transit, and social services.

Public hospitals, momentarily, had been spared the worst cuts after pushback from the legislature. Reductions to state agencies would be particularly punishing, however, because Cuomo had already spent a decade quietly gutting them. The State Department of Labor, straining to manage an onslaught of unemployment claims, had suffered a 28 percent decline in staffing from the 2011 to 2019 fiscal years.[140]

Laid off and furloughed New Yorkers were waiting weeks—and in some cases months—for unemployment benefits to arrive.

"I've reached out on Twitter. They said I would be contacted but still nothing," said Lynn Sakyiama, a Long Island resident who had failed to receive unemployment insurance after repeatedly trying to contact DOL. "I live paycheck to paycheck. I have no savings, and I spent my tax return on supplies for my child and my elderly parents. I just want to survive."[141]

Cuomo's posture however, had the potential to trigger another humanitarian disaster in the state. For the bulk of the pandemic, tenants were able to avoid evictions because a moratorium, under pressure from the Democrat-controlled legislature, was extended until at least May 2021. But Cuomo himself hadn't supported any programs to forgive or cut down on the rent burden, piling into the billions, that New York tenants would owe. By one estimate, there were at least a million tenants across the state who owed back rent.[142]

"In order to prevent massive economic disaster, our legislature must clear the back rent owed by New Yorkers and create a hardship fund for small landlords struggling to keep their buildings safe and afloat," Housing Justice for All, a coalition of more than 70 organizations across the state, said in a statement at the close of 2020.

★ ★ ★

The seeds for the current eviction crisis in New York had been planted decades earlier—and Cuomo had done little, for most of his time in office, to prevent it from happening. In the middle of the 20th century, New York City enjoyed both economic growth and a boom in affordable housing construction, including the New York City Housing Authority developments and numerous rent-stabilized and rent-controlled apartment buildings.

A substantial majority of New Yorkers lived in apartment units subject to the whims of the free market and the landlord, with no right to renew a lease and no protections against astronomical rent hikes. These New Yorkers were the unlucky majority. However, alongside NYCHA residents, who lived in affordable and relatively dignified housing until it fell into severe disrepair after the reduction of federal funding in the latter half of the 20th century, a significant minority could enjoy a rent-stabilized apartment, with rent increases governed by a city-run Rent Guidelines Board.

There were once hundreds of thousands more rent-stabilized apartments scattered across New York City than there are today. Until 1994, the nearly 900,000 apartments that were rent-stabilized had to remain forever in the program, their rent increases capped annually. For tenants, this meant a certain level of comfort and predictability because the Rent Guidelines Board would usually vote for miniscule increases. The city's median rent in 1994 was below $600 and apartments could be had in neighborhoods like the Lower East Side for $552 a month. For landlords, the long-sought goal had always been the end of all rent regulations in New York City: every apartment on the free market, the rent as high as the wealthiest tenant might pay.[143]

By the 1990s, landlords and real estate developers had grown restless, ready to take advantage of the city's rising economic fortunes. With the help of some liberal Democrats on the City Council and the conservative Democratic speaker, Peter Vallone, the Council voted to allow landlords to take apartments out of the rent stabilization system when the rent hit $2,000 a month. The Republican-controlled State Senate and George Pataki, the Republican governor, gladly signed off on the new law. The conversion would be called "vacancy decontrol."

At the time, landlords and many Democrats argued there were too many allegedly wealthy renters taking advantage of artificially low rents. Few people would ever pay $2,000 to live in neighborhoods like Bushwick or Bedford-Stuyvesant, they said.

The market would prove them wrong. Of the 860,000 apartments that were stabilized in 1994, almost 250,000 had become free-market units two decades later. In the same Lower East Side building with apartments under $600, rent exceeded $4,000 a month by the end of the 2010s.

Predatory landlords aggressively raised rent in the late 1990s and 2000s, exceeding the $2,000 threshold through legal but dubious means like performing unnecessary repairs or renovations on rental units or entire buildings. The beauty of rent-stabilization, if implemented on a mass scale, was that it is an ideal bulwark against displacement. Rents only rise so high. With stabilization eroded, gentrification could take flight.

Progressive Democrats tried repeatedly, in the 2000s and well into the 2010s, to end vacancy decontrol. Restoring the units lost was not a possibility, at least over the short-term, but if the remaining rent-stabilized units could stay that way for good, the bleeding could be staunched.

For obvious reasons, real estate developers and landlords enjoyed the status quo. If a building was rent-stabilized, a landlord merely had to harass tenants into vacating the apartments and then egregiously hike the rent. Converting a rent-stabilized unit into a "luxury" condominium—add a few new light fixtures, a remodeled kitchen and flooring—could be done quickly and marketed to upscale tenants.

These landlords were Cuomo's allies and Cuomo was the governor of big real estate. One 2018 analysis found that Cuomo had received more than $12 million in donations from the real estate industry since he took office in 2011.[144] These donors relied on Cuomo to hold the line against progressive Democrats who, at minimum, wanted to change the law so that apartments could no longer leave the rent-stabilization system. In the long run, time wasn't on the real estate industry's side—the state was adding Democrats to its voter rolls, progressives were growing more powerful and organized, and Cuomo could only do so much if legislators sent bills to his desk.

For a long time, they didn't. In 2011, with Cuomo's blessing, a group of four conservative Democrats in the State Senate broke away to form a third conference called the Independent Democratic Conference. In 2012, shortly after Democrats thought they had won enough seats to take the majority at last, the IDC announced it was joining with the Republicans to form an unprecedented power-sharing agreement—together, they would control the Senate, locking out the mainline Democrats.

Cuomo encouraged the IDC-Republican alliance. Publicly, he professed neutrality, writing it off as a problem of the legislature. Privately, he was greatly supportive, offering advice to the IDC on tactics and messaging. Top Cuomo aides helped broker the union.[145]

The practical outcome was more time—ultimately, another five years—of pro-tenant Democrats in the minority, unable to advance bills. The loopholes in New York's rent laws could not be fixed. Landlords were actively encouraged to allow their buildings to fall into disrepair or simply initiate wildly-disruptive construction projects that would force tenants, unable to tolerate the noise, dust, or collapsing infrastructure, to vacate their apartments.

"I was sitting at my desk, and the ceiling came down on top of me and my computer," recalled a Lower East Side rent-stabilized tenant in 2015.[146]

Michael McKee, a longtime New York housing activist, had tried repeatedly to get Cuomo to take housing rights issues more seriously. "As governor he has consistently refused to advocate for or use his power for stronger rent laws," McKee said. "He is not a progressive, not in the least progressive as far as I am concerned. He is certainly not a progressive Democrat. He will never be anything different."

Cuomo thwarting the pro-tenant Democrats in the State Senate meant that, with each passing year, more and more apartments could exit the rent-stabilization program. These were apartments that would never be available to future working-class tenants. Precarity, instead of stability, would be their reality.

In 2018, riding a national blue wave, Democrats drove Republicans from the State Senate majority. Six out of eight IDC members were defeated by progressive primary challengers. A year later, in 2019, the new Democratic majority united, over Cuomo's quiet resistance, to strengthen tenant protections and make it illegal for rent-stabilized units to leave the program.

But, over Cuomo's decade, the damage had already been done. "Nine more years of evictions and rent-gouging. Nine more years of a loss of affordable housing," McKee said. "Just like a hemorrhage which he did nothing to stop."[147]

By the time the COVID-19 pandemic ravaged New York, those who lived in rent-stabilized units had certain safeguards against evictions. But there could have been many more apartments protected under the program, if only Cuomo had taken action years earlier.

It was a cost that, on one hand, could seem invisible. Physical apartments don't vanish. Entire buildings don't suddenly crumble into sand. Rather, there are histories, hidden from view, that have grown all too common in Cuomo's New York.

The beleaguered tenant pleading for mercy with the landlord. Eviction notices slapped on paint-chipped doors. Housing courts overrun with cases.

All of it, too, was bound to become more visible when evictions, forestalled during the pandemic, could proceed again. Renters were maxing out credit cards and burning through savings to stay in their homes. The unemployed, sliding further into debt, were nearing destitution, if they weren't there already. They were cutting back on food and forgoing doctor visits. Families were piling into apartments, doubling and tripling up.

It was life lived on a grim, terrifying margin.

For all the strength of New York's newer tenant protections, there was the reality that a lease represented a contract that could not be readily voided—and landlords would demand their cash.

Cuomo had not advocated for any kind of mass bailout of renters, though Democrats in the legislature had. A moratorium would mean little if it was only putting off the day that hundreds of thousands, if not more, would trudge to housing court. By the start of 2021, as many as 1.2 million people across New York State were at risk for eviction.[148]

Tenants were never of great concern to Cuomo. They were not a constituency with money—they weren't showing up at his fundraisers—and their demands conflicted with those in the real estate industry who had a direct line to the governor's office. In his 2021 State of the State address, delivered in January, Cuomo merely offered to prohibit penalties and late fees on past due rent. These fees represented a miniscule fraction of the money tenants would be forced to pay to landlords in the spring. A top tenant advocate, Cea Weaver, called Cuomo's proposal a "cruel joke."[149]

Weaver and others demanded Cuomo cancel the growing rent debt. It was a proposal he never seemed to take seriously, despite the suffering that awaited.

★ ★ ★

By the summer of 2020, a new game of chicken commenced. Cuomo began to demand, rightfully, that the federal government step up to assist New York and save the state budget. But the federal government was controlled by Donald Trump, a president who had little interest in assisting Democrat-run states. The Republican majority leader, Mitch McConnell, referred to local aid as a "blue state bailout," refusing the Democrat-controlled House's attempts to funnel more cash to individual states as the pandemic worsened.

Democrats in New York, recognizing the hostility in Washington, begged Cuomo to allow them to raise taxes instead. "It's bullshit. Don't wait for Donald Trump," said Jessica Ramos, a Democratic state senator, at the start of summer. "I get the feeling our congressional delegation feels the same way. The fact is, waiting for a psychopath with no empathy to actually be responsive to our needs is a mistake."[150]

In the pandemic spring and summer, Cuomo demanded federal aid. But it was clear to anyone even dimly aware of the political situation in Washington, that the aid would not be forthcoming. What was stranger—or, perhaps, intentional—was Cuomo's refusal to consider any other revenue sources. The Federal Reserve had set up the Municipal Liquidity Facility to provide low interest loans to struggling cities and states. In the fall, the Metropolitan Transportation Authority, warning of doomsday cuts, borrowed $2.9 billion from the Fed, but no other state agency or locality took advantage of the program. Cuomo didn't reference it much publicly, if he referenced it at all.

More promising for many Democrats in the legislature and activists on the left were tax hikes on the rich. New York was home to more than 100 billionaires and many more multimillionaires. Republican and Democratic governors alike had turned to tax hikes in previous economic downturns, quickly raising the funds needed to forestall deeper austerity. In the wake of the 2008 economic crash, David Paterson had signed off on a "millionaire's tax" and an MTA payroll tax to help raise funds. George Pataki, the Republican who defeated Mario Cuomo, was forced to accept post-9/11 tax hikes after the state legislature overrode his veto. Before him, Nelson Rockefeller, another Republican governor, had raised income taxes during a recession.

Cuomo, however, was willing to break with all precedent. The rich could not be taxed, he insisted repeatedly.

"I literally talk to people all day long who are in their Hamptons house who also lived here, or in their Hudson Valley house or in their Connecticut weekend house, and I say, 'You gotta come back, when are you coming back?'" Cuomo said in August, in response to yet another question about why he refused to consider raising taxes. "They're not coming back right now. And you know what else they're thinking? If I stay there,

I pay a lower income tax because they don't pay the New York City surcharge."

The argument was especially disingenuous because legislators and activists were calling for various statewide surcharges, not those just for New York City. A millionaire in the Hamptons or the Hudson Valley would still have to pay. A year earlier, when asked about raising taxes in a far more promising economic environment, Cuomo was just as dismissive: "I don't believe in raising taxes on the rich. That would be the worst thing to do. You would just expand the shortfall," he said. "God forbid if the rich leave."[151]

A new "millionaire's tax" more than a decade ago hadn't chased the masters of the universe out of New York. But Cuomo, who drew a bulk of his political donations from the finance and real estate sectors, was sensitive to their complaints—few ultrawealthy like paying high taxes, after all. The federal aid that Cuomo demanded, however, was not arriving. Not in the summer, not in the fall, not in the winter—not as long as Trump sat in the White House.

In September, the Democratic governor of New Jersey, Phil Murphy, announced that he had struck a deal with the legislature to raise taxes on those earning more than $1 million. "We do not hold any grudge at all against those who have been successful in life, but in this unprecedented time when so many middle class families and others have sacrificed so much, now is the time to ensure that the wealthiest among us are also called to sacrifice," Murphy said.

New York state's budget office estimated in October that coronavirus was responsible for a $13.5 billion drop in state revenue from its February projections. The state projected an $8.7 billion deficit for the next fiscal year, a sum with little precedent.

Instead of raising taxes, Cuomo was content to wait, allowing Mujica to effectively slash spending to levels not seen in decades. Some of the cuts fell hardest on education, both K-12 public schools and the public university systems, particularly the state-run City University of New York. Before the pandemic, state aid to CUNY, adjusted for inflation, had declined by nearly 5 percent during Cuomo's tenure, though the state's gross domestic product had increased. New York's Tuition Assistance Program, which provided aid to students below a certain income threshold, no longer covered the full cost of tuition, and Cuomo had forced individual colleges to make up the difference.[152]

In early 2016, in a far better economic climate, Cuomo attempted to slash state aid to CUNY by nearly $500 million. After encountering furious backlash, Cuomo reluctantly backed off. A few months later, however, he appointed Mujica to the CUNY Board of Trustees, consolidating the executive branch's control over the university system.

CUNY, a system that serves a largely nonwhite, low-income student population—42 percent of all first-time freshmen come from households with incomes of $20,000 or less—had been a victim of austerity for decades, first drained of funds when New York City nearly went bankrupt in the 1970s. Forty-five years later, a devastating repeat appeared likely as Mujica began slashing state spending by as much as 20 percent to public colleges and universities.

First, 2,800 adjuncts were laid off. Those that remained, especially non-teaching adjuncts that worked in other areas of the colleges, like libraries, saw steep reductions in their hours. Courses disappeared, ballooning class sizes for the fall semester. A mathematics lecture class at City College in Manhattan that, in a normal year, would seat less than 50 now had more than 70 students.

Individual colleges operated on month-to-month budgets, unheard of in a system that always had a fiscal year budget to work from. Faculty chairs were told to create schedules for future semesters with only full-time faculty slotted for classes. In typical years, adjuncts would receive reappointments and be assigned classes for the upcoming semester.

"The administration is just trying to make payroll and as we go deeper into the school year, it will be harder to make payroll. At some point, they are going to have to go deep into adjunct cuts," said James Davis, an English professor and deputy chair for graduate studies at Brooklyn College, in October. "People are freaking out or getting fired."[153]

What made Cuomo's austerity inordinately punishing and disorienting was how hidden it turned out to be. Ordinary budget cuts are announced; leadership grimly informs the populace that times are difficult and reductions must be made. Funding for schools, hospitals and agencies will be cut by *this much* on *this particular date*, the executive declares. Budget documents are produced that attest to the misery to come.

No such documents were forthcoming during New York's first year in the pandemic. By the end of 2020, Cuomo and Mujica had not announced any formal budget cuts or produced publicly available documents to explain exactly how much state funding had been reduced and which agencies and areas had been impacted most.

It was fog-of-war austerity; a school district in Schenectady, anticipating a loss of aid, could suddenly lay off hundreds of teachers and staff with no warning. Mujica had floated 20 percent reductions everywhere—but whether some school districts, the MTA, or other state agencies suffered even more than these cuts (which weren't even being called cuts by the state) was unclear to everyone, including reporters, state lawmakers, and advocacy organizations.

"The longer that the State withholds payments, the more likely they are to become de facto cuts as recipients manage their activities without funds or certainty of receipt," wrote a collective of good government and advocacy groups to Mujica at the end of December.[154]

Other local funding had already been declining under Cuomo, despite New York's economic growth over the last decade. Spending on state human services, including aid to help localities pay for public assistance, was slashed by 26 percent between the 2011 and 2018 fiscal years.[155] The ongoing reduction in state local aid had meant counties had fewer resources to properly fund human services, including mental health and public health.

In the new year, state lawmakers promised to vote to raise taxes. Cuomo, even, seemed increasingly open to such a deal. "We're going to have to raise taxes—I believe we're going to have to raise taxes, at the end of the day, in any event," Cuomo said in December. "The question is, how much in tax?"

Cuomo's embrace of austerity during the pandemic reflected his fundamentally neoliberal worldview. Government could only do so much to protect the working class and poor from the forces of the market. The rich should not be taxed aggressively to more equally distribute wealth. In 2020, a tax hike would not impact the ultrawealthy, thanks to Cuomo. Government was shrinking, and shrinking on his terms.

But the progressives in his state were rising, far more willing to stand up to him in the legislature and in the media. The GOP-aligned Independent Democratic Conference, in part a Cuomo creation, was vanquished in 2018, and all the primary challengers who replaced them backed many of the priorities that had long been anathema to a fiscally conservative governor. In 2020, several outwardly socialist politicians were elected to the state legislature, with other leftists joining them.

On the day Biden defeated Trump, Democrats were still crushed in downballot races across America, losing seats in the House of Representatives and failing to retake state legislatures in crucial states like Ohio, Michigan, Pennsylvania, and Florida. In New York, the election also appeared devastating for

Democrats, with some Trump-supporting Republicans holding strong leads in the vote count.

The likelihood of this pattern repeating in New York was increased by the intervention of Ronald Lauder, the billionaire cosmetics heir, and a close enough friend of Cuomo's that he once allowed the governor to fly back on his private plane after taking a trip to Poland. With Cuomo's tacit blessing, Lauder poured millions into television advertisements attacking vulnerable Senate Democrats for supporting criminal justice reforms, including a partial end to cash bail.

New York had an inordinate number of absentee ballots to be tabulated because of the pandemic. Unlike **in** those other states, New York's Board of Elections was patronage-ridden and deeply dysfunctional because Cuomo had never attempted to reform an election apparatus that dated back to the machine-driven politics of the 19th century. State law didn't permit absentee ballots to be counted until many days after Election Day.

The count was protracted and exhausting, and New York was the last state in America to certify its election results. For progressives, however, the long wait was worth it. Democrats in the State Senate gained sufficient seats to form a supermajority with enough members to finally be able to override one of Cuomo's vetoes. Many of the new state senators were proud leftists, championing tax hikes on the rich and universal healthcare. None appeared cowed by Cuomo. His long reign with untrammeled power in the state was over.

CONCLUSION
AN END TO THE CUOMO SHOW?

In Cuomo's mind, there was no need for redemption when it came to his handling of the COVID-19 pandemic. He had succeeded, somehow, even on a mountaintop of death. Even despite the fact that coronavirus cases spiked again at the start of 2021 and a fresh, more transmissible strain of the virus, known as the UK Strain—or B.1.1.7.—appeared in many states, including New York. Hospitals were tested again, though not to the apocalyptic levels of the spring.

This time, however, New York and America had a weapon to combat the surge. Two vaccines, one developed by Pfizer and their partner BioNTech and the other by Moderna, became available by the end of 2020. For the very first time during the pandemic, hope was tangible. Soon, millions could have immunity against coronavirus.

On December 14, an intensive care nurse named Sandra Lindsay sat in front of television cameras, her left arm exposed. A needle entered her arm with the new vaccine. On screen was Cuomo, smiling and applauding from his office. Lindsay, a nurse at Long Island Jewish Medical Center, on the border between New York City and Nassau County, was the first person in the country to be vaccinated for coronavirus. The hospital, not coincidentally, belonged to the Northwell Health system, which enjoyed an unusually close relationship with the governor.

"This is the light at the end of the tunnel," Cuomo said. "But it's a long tunnel."

At that moment, New Yorkers could be forgiven for believing that, soon enough, doses of the new vaccines would flood the state. Instead of opting to vaccinate senior citizens first—statistically, they were far more likely to die of the virus—Cuomo decided, like many other governors across America, to develop complex regulations that would prioritize healthcare workers and nursing home residents first.

To see a long-term decline in cases, public health experts estimated 10 to 20 percent of New York City's population would have to be vaccinated, as long as social distancing measures were still followed. But in the weeks after the first dose of the vaccine entered Lindsay's left arm, the city was nowhere close to that goal, let alone the state as a whole.

In the first 17 days of the vaccine rollout—from the joyous day at Long Island Jewish Medical Center to the start of the new year—just 88,140 people had received the first of two doses, the equivalent of about 1 percent of the city's population. Those vaccinated had overwhelmingly been hospital employees, residents, nursing home workers, and staff at certain health clinics.[156]

Mayor de Blasio and city officials wanted to move faster, but they were stymied. Cuomo, as always, had statewide rules that forbade local governments from following plans they had already devised to distribute the vaccine most effectively. Healthcare providers that gave out vaccines to those not deemed eligible under Cuomo's criteria were threatened with million dollar fines.

Cuomo's government developed a stringent matrix for who could receive a shot and when. Not only were vaccines restricted to healthcare workers and nursing home residents—the state instructed healthcare centers to vaccinate their employees in a specific order according to risk, job description, the environment the employee worked in, and how old they were, among other factors.

This approach was well-intentioned but soon turned out to be overly precise and confusing. Part of the problem lay in how Cuomo bypassed local health departments, which had developed vaccination plans and were ready to distribute doses at schools, churches, firehouses, and other public gathering places.

Many of the vaccines were restricted to hospitals, with no-one else able to use them. While it was understandable that Cuomo wanted to give vaccines to healthcare workers and nursing home residents, it made little sense to be so punitive and parsimonious with shots when the pandemic was still such a threat. Doses sat in New York City freezers so long that some were tossed out altogether.

Under pressure from de Blasio and various other Democrats—the New York City public advocate, Jumaane Williams, urged de Blasio to violate state law and start distributing unused doses immediately—Cuomo finally relented, expanding vaccine access to all people 75 and over. Shortly after, the criteria were expanded to all senior citizens.

Large city- and state-run vaccination sites were established quickly. De Blasio's Health Department, however, devised a website that was exceedingly challenging for senior citizens to use, forcing them to answer 51 questions, upload images of their insurance cards, and have an email to receive a QR code. Scott Stringer, the city comptroller and a top candidate for mayor, fumed that "we've set up a gauntlet that requires tech support."

A new problem soon arose, one for which neither Cuomo nor de Blasio—for all their incompetence—could be blamed: a lack of vaccine. Trump's federal government, and then Biden's, could not provide enough doses to meet pent-up demand in New York and elsewhere. City-run sites and local hospitals began canceling appointments. By the end of January scheduling one at all, on a city website or at a pharmacy, became virtually impossible.

With the Biden government vowing to rev up distribution of the vaccine and a third, from Johnson & Johnson deployed for emergency use in February, relief appeared to be on the way. Yet it is worth considering why, in the crucial period of

December, New York allowed any doses at all to go to waste. Other states, including Connecticut, Massachusetts, and West Virginia were able to vaccinate at a faster rate. Their governors declined the opportunity to appear regularly on national television or published pandemic memoirs. They just got on with the job of delivering the vaccine in a more efficient manner than New York under its media-obsessed governor.

★ ★ ★

In his seminal work, *Amusing Ourselves to Death*, the media theorist Neil Postman warned of a dark fusion of news and entertainment. Writing in the 1980s, when a former movie actor had ascended to the White House, Postman despaired over the dominance of television, and how information relayed through a screen would naturally shed the nuance required to properly comprehend government, politics, and society writ large. Television, Postman wrote, "serves us most usefully when presenting junk-entertainment; it serves us most ill when it co-opts serious modes of discourse—news, politics, science, education, commerce, religion—and turns them into entertainment packages."[157]

On Friday, November 20, 2020, the International Academy of Television Arts and Sciences announced it would set a precedent in presenting its Founders Award, traditionally given to industry executives who had crossed "cultural boundaries to touch our common humanity."

In the past, actors and actresses playing fictional politicians—Selina Meyer, Josiah Bartlet—had won Emmys. Al Gore had accepted the Founders Award in 2007, but by then he was no longer vice president; he was not recognized for governing, but for launching a television network: Current TV. Now, the academy announced, a politician holding an elected office could finally claim the International Emmy Founders Award.

Step forward Andrew Cuomo.

"The Governor's 111 daily briefings worked so well because he effectively created television shows, with characters, plot lines, and stories of success and failure," the academy's president and CEO, Bruce Paisner, explained in a statement. "People around the world tuned in to find out what was going on, and *New York tough* became a symbol of the determination to fight back."

A few days later, Cuomo accepted the award.

"I wish I could say that my daily COVID presentations are well-choreographed, scripted, rehearsed, or reflected any of the talents you advance. They didn't," Cuomo said in pre-taped remarks. "They offered only one thing: authentic truth and stability. But sometimes that's enough."

Four years after Donald Trump won a black swan presidential election, the merger of news and entertainment had reached yet another perverse apotheosis. A virus had killed tens of thousands of New Yorkers, ravaging America's largest city like no crisis before it. Untold thousands were grieving losses they would never recover from. Of the living, more than a million were unemployed. The September 11 attacks would always be a singular trauma, but the localized effect of coronavirus—in lives lost, in livelihoods ruined—would far outstrip that single day. Like total war, it had impacted everyone. Like total war, the horror lingered, the terminus never quite clear. A vaccine was coming. But people kept dying.

Inarguably, Trump failed the nation. He denied the threat of coronavirus. He needlessly politicized mask-wearing and egged on anti-lockdown protests. He didn't coordinate a serious response among states. He had no national testing strategy. He rejected a federal role in tracing and isolating infections. He didn't ban travel from Europe quickly enough. He was too hesitant to invoke the Defense Production Act to ensure a stream of necessary equipment to hospitals.

Individual governors ignored science too. Republicans like Ron DeSantis of Florida and Kristi Noem of South Dakota flaunted public health guidance. Too many states failed to implement face-covering mandates until it was too late. California, after its early action to stem the spread of the virus, reopened too quickly. Gavin Newsom's state would be battered by second and third waves. By the end of 2020, Southern California was the American epicenter, and in 2021, California's death toll at last surpassed New York's. Still, the death rate in New York remained far higher, because California is more than double its size.

America wasn't alone either. The United Kingdom, at times, had a higher death rate, as did Italy and Spain. The real success stories were in the eastern hemisphere, in places like Vietnam, Taiwan, and South Korea. No matter how prudent a state or nation's particular leadership was, containing coronavirus was a daunting task. Even Germany, held up as a European ideal, encountered another crippling wave as winter set in.

But there were certain facts it was impossible to ignore: the earlier a locality moved to enact social distancing measures in the first weeks and months of the pandemic, the easier it became to save lives. Washington State limited fatalities by acting promptly. While coronavirus tore through Southern California, San Francisco's early prudence paid off. Well into 2021, less than 500 residents had died of coronavirus there, compared to the 30,000 dead in New York City.

The dreadful scale of death in New York, nearly 50,000 lost at the time of writing, was not inevitable. Governonr Cuomo was too slow to shut down his state. He compared coronavirus to the flu and downplayed the threat. He failed to adequately coordinate hospitals to handle the surge of patients.

The plaudits he won for containing the virus were undeserved because they followed so much preventable death. And once the caseload decreased from its catastrophic peak, he slashed services for the working class and poor, inflicting still more suffering.

For as long as anyone could remember, the media had been good to Cuomo. The most famous governor in the nation charmed millions of viewers with his televised briefings, reciting bare facts from his homely PowerPoints. Journalists, pundits and cable television hosts swooned. The Cuomo myth grew in proportion to the bodies piling up in hospital morgues. It lingered beyond any point of rationality. Many months after the peak of suffering in New York, a journalist with *New York Magazine* could state to Cuomo, without irony, "You've been criticized in retrospect for moving too slowly, but you actually got to a shutdown pretty quickly."[158] This mythic Cuomo never made sense to those who had covered the pandemic closely and investigated the opaque workings of the government he controlled. For a long time, though, that didn't seem to matter. The biggest media companies in America had their plot lines to write. Inconvenient facts, like immunity shields and hidden nursing home death counts and early comparisons to the flu, were left on the cutting-room floor.

As spring 2021 arrived in New York, Cuomo returned to the center of the media universe. But it was not like before. This time, at least six women accused him of sexual harassment. This time, the FBI launched an investigation into his administration's oversight of nursing homes. This time, a state legislator named Ron Kim who went public with threats Cuomo made against him became famous too. This time, almost every politician of note in New York—Chuck Schumer, Kirsten Gillibrand, Alexandria Ocasio-Cortez, and Andrea Stewart-Cousins— called for him to resign. The State Assembly, once so cautious and plodding, opened an impeachment investigation.

Cuomo was on the front page of every New York City newspaper, a headliner of the nightly newscasts, and a constant subject of debate and intrigue on CNN and MSNBC. Corporate media abhorred a vacuum. If Trump had still been president of the United States, Cuomo could count on the idiocy and scandal in the White House to distract from whatever came out of New York.

That's how he became a star in the first place. Trump's federal response to the pandemic was so plainly horrendous, any questions about failure on the local level could always be deflected, especially by blinkered, Cuomo-worshiping Democrats. One salacious, incendiary, or perplexing Trump tweet could seize a headline and give cover to all of those who, like Cuomo, were failing out of view.

Those days were now gone. Joe Biden, a conventional Democrat, was president. He did not like to tweet. He did not feud with the media, celebrities, Democrats, or even most Republicans. Trump had left the stage, his rantings confined to occasional Fox News appearances. The major media companies needed new scandals to occupy their viewers, to seize their imaginations and keep them coming back for more. They lacked the self-awareness to interrogate what exactly they were doing—daily excoriating a man they had once portrayed as an American hero—but they were, at least, acting as accountable journalists, a role that they had abdicated a year earlier.

Cuomo was dying on the sword he once lived by. The Cuomo scandals were perfect for cable TV because they were both legitimate and compelling. There was a natural narrative arc, a rising and falling action; media companies and newspapers helped create a myth, and now they would tear it down. This was the fate a television character as abhorrent as Cuomo deserved. He was huddled in his Albany mansion, pining for a comeback arc. But his cancellation was just as likely.

All of the converging currents of scandal—the alleged lurid behavior towards women, the nursing home data cover-ups—sprang from a culture of impunity that had been endemic, in retrospect, to the whole Cuomo enterprise. He attacked because he could. He lied because he could. The glue that bound Cuomo's machine was fear. He operated, in the purest sense, from Machiavelli's dictum that it is better to be feared than loved. Over the last decade, he publicly and privately denigrated many of the politicians who later turned on him simply because he *could*—everyone, in Cuomo's universe, always needed to be reminded of their place.

But what would happen when none of these people were any longer afraid of Cuomo? There was no lingering goodwill, no loyalty tied to the implicit transaction—*I am powerful, and I can choose either to help you or destroy you.*

Bruce Paisner, the academy president who announced Cuomo's Emmy, was right in one sense. The governor had, indeed, created television shows with characters, plot lines, and stories of success and failure. He had crafted his own reality, and millions gladly accepted it. They were ordinary people looking for guidance in a time of fear. They were also journalists, pundits, and political operatives who knew better. Cuomo had been cast as a hero because the villain was so plain: Trump, the most deranged executive anyone remembered. The federal response had been so inept, so disastrous that it *demanded* a foil—those are the rules of narrative and entertainment, right?

But foils only survive as long as they have forces, larger even than themselves, to work against. In 2021, after inciting a riot at the Capitol, Trump left the White House, his Twitter account deactivated, his idiocy no longer consuming the national discourse. He no longer offered cover for the arrogance, venality, and ineptitude practiced by politicians he outranked. In the era beyond Trump, Cuomo would have to answer for the catastrophe in New York. He would be alone, the facts laid bare. More than a million confirmed cases. Nearly 50,000 dead. This was the legacy he would leave behind, and, at last, for which he would be held accountable.

NOTES

1. "Pneumonia of Unknown Cause—China," World Health Organization, published January 5, 2020, https://www.who.int/csr/don/05-january-2020-pneumonia-of-unkown-cause-china/en/.
2. Anna Palmer and Jake Sherman, "*Politico* Playbook: Popping the Bolton Bubble," Politico, published January 5, 2020, https://www.politico.com/newsletters/playbook/2020/01/07/popping-the-bolton-bubble-488002.
3. Joseph Spector, "New York State Budget Deal Reached: Everything You Need to Know," *Democrat and Chronicle*, published March 31, 2019, https://www.democratandchronicle.com/story/news/politics/albany/2019/03/31/new-york-state-budget-deal-reached-everything-you-need-know/3325062002/.
4. Jake Offenhartz, "Why is Cuomo Spending Over $200 Million on Fancy Bridge Lights as the MTA Crumbles?," Gothamist, published July 19, 2017, https://gothamist.com/news/why-is-cuomo-spending-over-200-million-on-fancy-bridge-lights-as-the-mta-crumbles.
5. Erin Durkin, "Cuomo Announces Major Penn Station Track Expansion," *Politico*, published January 6, 2020, https://www.politico.com/states/new-york/city-hall/story/2020/01/06/cuomo-announces-major-penn-station-track-expansion-1244539.
6. Richie Torres, "Gov. Cuomo: NY's Lyndon Johnson," *New York Daily News*, published April 23, 2018, https://www.nydailynews.com/opinion/gov-cuomo-n-y-s-lyndon-johnson-article-1.3946235.
7 "Siena College Poll," Siena Research Institute, published November 21, 2019, https://scri.siena.edu/wp-content/uploads/2019/11/SNY-November-2019-Poll-Release-11-21-19-FINAL.pdf.
8. Scottie Andrew and Giulia McDonnell Nieto del Rio, "NY Gov. Andrew Cuomo Came across a Car Accident and Cut a Man Loose from His Seat

NOTES

Belt, CNN, published January 6, 2020, https://www.cnn.com/2020/01/06/politics/andrew-cuomo-pulls-passenger-car-accident-trnd/index.html.

9. Lauren Gambino, "Ebola Nurse 'Made to Feel Like Criminal' on Return to US," *The Guardian*, published October 25, 2014, https://www.theguardian.com/world/2014/oct/25/obama-facts-not-fear-public-response-ebola-usa.

10.. Michael Schaub, "Andrew Cuomo Got $738,000 for His Memoir—and It Sold Only 3,200 Copies," *Los Angeles Times*, published April 19, 2017, https://www.latimes.com/books/jacketcopy/la-et-jc-andrew-cuomo-book-20170419-story.html.

11. Sydney Brownstone, Paige Cornwell, Mike Lindblom, and Elise Takahama, "Kings County Patient is First in US to Die of COVID-19 as Officials Scramble to Stem Spread of Novel Coronavirus," *The Seattle Times*, published February 29, 2020, https://www.seattletimes.com/seattle-news/health/one-king-county-patient-has-died-due-to-covid-19-infection/.

12. Jamie Ducharme and Jasmine Aguilera, "Coronavirus Containment Efforts in the US Could Disrupt 'People's Day-to-Day Lives,' CDC Warns," *Time Magazine*, published February 25, 2020, https://time.com/5790368/coronavirus-community-spread-us/.

13. Charles Duhigg, "Seattle's Leaders Let Scientists Take the Lead. New York's Did Not," *The New Yorker*, published April 26, 2020, https://www.newyorker.com/magazine/2020/05/04/seattles-leaders-let-scientists-take-the-lead-new-yorks-did-not.

14. Karen Weise, "Ahead of the Pack, How Microsoft Told Workers to Stay Home," the *New York Times*, published March 15, 2020, https://www.nytimes.com/2020/03/15/technology/microsoft-coronavirus-response.html.

15. Megan Campbell, "Dow Constantine Calls on Businesses, Individuals to Slow the Spread of COVID-19, *Puget Sound Business Journal*, published March 4, 2020, https://www.bizjournals.com/seattle/news/2020/03/04/dow-constantine-calls-on-businesses-individuals-to.html.

16. Marshall Cohen, Christopher Hickey, and Tara Subraniam, "The Lost Month," CNN, published April 18, 2020, https://www.cnn.com/interactive/2020/04/politics/trump-covid-response-annotation/.

17. Julia Belluz, "Is It Safe to Travel during the Coronavirus Outbreak? An Infectious Disease Specialist Explains," Vox Media, published January 29, 2020, https://www.vox.com/2020/1/29/21113282/coronavirus-travel-ban-advisory-china-is-it-safe.

18. US Surgeon General (Jerome Adams), Twitter, published March 2, 2020 (has since been deleted).

19. "Governor Cuomo Delivers Update on Novel Coronavirus," Youtube video, Andrew Cuomo, published February 29, 2020, https://www.youtube.com/watch?v=UHxm2QHNv3g.

20. WRGB Staff, "Focus on the Flu, Not the Coronavirus Urges Gov. Cuomo," WRGB Albany, published February 7, 2020, https://cbs6albany.com/news/local/focus-on-the-flu-not-the-coronavirus-urges-gov-cuomo.

21. Andrew Cuomo, *American Crisis: Leadership Lessons from the COVID-19 Pandemic*, (New York: Crown Publishing Group, 2020) 19–20.

22. Cuomo, *American Crisis*, 20.

23. "Gov. Cuomo and NYC Mayor de Blasio Speak on New York Coronavirus Case," Youtube video, CNBC, published March 2, 2020, https://www.youtube.com/watch?v=Kub_giTgbvY.

24. Bill de Blasio, Twitter, published March 2, 2020, https://twitter.com/BilldeBlasio/status/1234648718714036229.

25. Nina Shapiro, "Six People Have Now Died from Coronavirus Disease in Washington State; King County Buying a Motel to House Isolated Patients," *The Seattle Times*, published March 2, 2020, https://www.seattletimes.com/seattle-news/health/king-county-now-has-14-coronavirus-cases-including-5-deaths/.

26. Mike Carter, "New Coronavirus Cases in Western Washington Are Likely Doubling Every Six Days, Fred Hutch Scientist Says," *The Seattle Times*, updated March 3, 2020, https://www.seattletimes.com/seattle-news/health/new-coronavirus-cases-in-western-washington-are-likely-doubling-every-6-days-fred-hutch-scientist-says/.

27. "Fox's Dr. Marc Siegel Says 'Worst Case Scenario' for Coronavirus Is 'It Could Be the Flu,'" Media Matters, published March 6, 2020, https://www.mediamatters.org/sean-hannity/foxs-dr-marc-siegel-says-worse-case-scenario-coronavirus-it-could-be-flu.

NOTES

28. Reality Check Team, "Coronavirus: How is the Chinese City at the Centre of the Outbreak Coping?" BBC News, published January 24, 2020, https://www.bbc.com/news/world-asia-51224504.

29. Cuomo, *American Crisis*, 25–26.

30. Joseph Spector, "Containment Area in New Rochelle Because of Coronavirus: What You Need to Know," *The Journal News*, published March 10, 2020, https://www.lohud.com/story/news/politics/2020/03/10/containment-zone-new-rochelle-national-guard-coronavirus-what-know/5012501002/.

31. Matt Papaycik, "DeSantis Says Spike in Coronavirus Cases Is Due to More Testing," WFLX, updated June 17, 2020, https://www.wflx.com/2020/06/16/desantis-says-spike-coronavirus-cases-is-due-more-testing/.

32. Benedict Carey and James Glanz, "Hidden Outbreaks Spread Through US Cities Far Earlier Than Americans Knew, Estimates Say," the *New York Times*, published April 23, 3030, https://www.nytimes.com/2020/04/23/us/coronavirus-early-outbreaks-cities.html?action=click&module=Spotlight&pgtype=Homepage.

33. Scott Gottlieb, Twitter, published March 7, 2020, https://twitter.com/ScottGottliebMD/status/1236473220783636481.

34. Ross Barkan, "Albany's Dead-of-Night Coronavirus Vote Gives Cuomo Sweeping New Emergency Powers," Gothamist, published March 5, 2020, https://gothamist.com/news/ny-coronavirus-cuomo-new-emergency-powers.

35. "Governor Cuomo Confirms 16 Additional Coronavirus Cases in New York State, Bringing Statewide Total to 105," Official Website of Governor Andrew M. Cuomo, published March 8, 2020, https://www.governor.ny.gov/news/video-b-roll-audio-photos-rush-transcript-governor-cuomo-confirms-16-additional-coronavirus.

36. Anemona Hartocollis and Marc Santora, "Plenty of Hugs as Craig Spencer, Recovered New York Ebola Patient, Goes Home," the *New York Times*, published November 11, 2014, https://www.nytimes.com/2014/11/12/nyregion/craig-spencer-new-york-ebola-patient-bellevue.html.

37. "Governor Cuomo Announces New York State Will Contract with 28 Private Labs to Increase Coronavirus Testing Capacity," Official Website of Governor Andrew M. Cuomo, published March 11, 2020, https://www. governor.ny.gov/news/video-audio-photos-rush-transcript-during-novel-coronavirus-briefing-governor-cuomo-announces.
38. Liam Stack, "St. Patrick's Day Parade Is Postponed in New York Over Coronavirus Concerns," the *New York Times*, published March 11, 2020, https://www.nytimes.com/2020/03/11/nyregion/new-york-st-patricks-day-parade-canceled.html.
39. Charles Duhigg, "Seattle's Leaders Let Scientists Take the Lead. New York's Did Not," *The New Yorker*, published April 26, 2020, https://www. newyorker.com/magazine/2020/05/04/seattles-leaders-let-scientists-take-the-lead-new-yorks-did-not.
40. Elizabeth Kim, "Coronavirus Updates: De Blasio Declares State of Emergency in NYC," Gothamist, published March 12, 2020, https:// gothamist.com/news/coronavirus-nyc-covid19-restrictions.
41. "During Novel Coronavirus Briefing, Governor Cuomo Announces New Mass Gatherings Regulations," Official Website of Governor Andrew M. Cuomo, published March 12, 2020, https://www.governor.ny.gov/news/ video-audio-photos-rush-transcript-during-novel-coronavirus-briefing-governor-cuomo-announces-0.
42. Dana Rubenstein, "Cuomo Continues His Ping-Pong Approach to Subway Ownership," *Politico*, published August 31, 2018, https://www. politico.com/states/new-york/albany/story/2018/08/31/cuomo-continues-his-ping-pong-approach-to-subway-ownership-588765.
43. Ross Barkan, "'We Have No Nurses and No Isolation Room,'" *The Nation*, published March 15, 2020, https://www.thenation.com/article/ society/coronavirus-schools-nyc/.
44. Glenn Coin, "Monroe County Closes All Schools Indefinitely," Syracuse. com, published March 14, 2020, https://www.syracuse.com/coronavirus/ 2020/03/monroe-county-closes-all-schools-indefinitely.html.
45. Elizabeth Kim, "Coronavirus Updates: De Blasio Outlines Plan to Build Out 8,200 Hospital Beds," Gothamist, published March 16, 2020, https:// gothamist.com/news/coronavirus-updates-monday-cuomo-catastrophe.

NOTES

46. Eve Batey, "California Governor Gavin Newsom Says All Bars and Wineries Should Close to Fight Spread of Coronavirus," Eater SF, published March 15, 2020, https://sf.eater.com/2020/3/15/21180845/california-coronavirus-bars-restaurants-newsom.

47. "Mayor De Blasio Holds Media Availability on COVID-19," Official Website of the City of New York, published March 15, 2020, https://www1.nyc.gov/office-of-the-mayor/news/150-20/mayor-de-blasio-holds-media-availability-covid-19.

48. Jake Offenhartz and Christopher Robbins, "With De Blasio's Blessing, NYC Nightlife Still Buzzing Despite Pleas to Self-Isolate," Gothamist, published March 15, 2020, https://gothamist.com/news/pandemic-at-the-disco-nyc-coronavirus-bars.

49. Erin Allday, "Bay Area Orders 'Shelter-in-Place,' Only Essential Businesses Open in 6 Counties," San Francisco Chronicle, published March 19, 2020, https://www.sfchronicle.com/local-politics/article/Bay-Area-must-shelter-in-place-Only-15135014.php.

50. Elizabeth Kim, "Coronavirus Updates: New York State Now Has More Than 1,500 Cases, Cuomo Says US Army Corps of Engineers Are Coming Wednesday," Gothamist, published March 17, 2020, https://gothamist.com/news/coronavirus-updates-de-blasio-nyc-stimulus-checks.

51. Cuomo, American Crisis, 92.

52. Chandelis Duster and Paul LeBlanc, "New York Governor Dismisses Possibility of Shelter-in-Place Order After Mayor Urged New Yorkers to Prepare for It," CNN, published March 17, 2020, https://www.cnn.com/2020/03/17/politics/bill-de-blasio-andrew-cuomo-new-york-shelter-in-place-coronavirus-cnntv/index.html.

53. Cuomo, American Crisis, 98.

54. Elizabeth Kim, "Coronavirus Updates: De Blasio Says He Wants Cuomo to Consider San Francisco's Shelter-in-Place Model," Gothamist, published March 18, 2020, https://gothamist.com/news/coronavirus-updates-de-blasio-and-cuomo-spar-over-shelter-place-order.

55. "Executive Order: Continuing Temporary Suspension and Modification of Laws Relating to the Disaster Emergency," Official Website of

Governor Andrew M. Cuomo, published March 18, 2020, https://www.governor.ny.gov/news/no-2025-continuing-temporary-suspension-and-modification-laws-relating-disaster-emergency.

56. Ben Smith, "Andrew Cuomo is the Control Freak We Need Right Now," the *New York Times*, published March 16, 2020, https://www.nytimes.com/2020/03/16/business/media/cuomo-new-york-coronavirus.html.

57. Mara Gay, Twitter, published March 17, 2020, https://twitter.com/MaraGay/status/1239927075152199681.

58. Rebecca Fishbein, "My Best Recollection of the Call I Just Had with Andrew Cuomo," Jezebel, published March 19, 2020, https://jezebel.com/my-best-recollection-of-the-call-i-just-had-with-andrew-1842416129.

59. "See Gov. Cuomo's Response When Asked About Running for President," CNN, published March 31, 2020, https://www.cnn.com/videos/politics/2020/03/31/governor-andrew-cuomo-run-for-president-cpt-vpx.cnn.

60. Elizabeth Kim, "Coronavirus Updates: NYC Will Run Out of Medical Supplies in 2–3 Weeks, De Blasio Says," published March 19, 2020, https://gothamist.com/news/coronavirus-updates-cuomo-shelter-in-place-scary.

61. Christopher Robbins, "Gov. Cuomo Announces Stay-at-Home Order: 'New York State On PAUSE," Gothamist, published March 20, 2020, https://gothamist.com/news/gov-cuomo-announces-stay-home-order-new-york-state-pause.

62. Cuomo, American Crisis, 103.

63. Eve Batey, "California Governor Gavin Newsom Says All Bars and Wineries Should Close to Fight Spread of Coronavirus," Eater SF, published March 15, 2020, https://sf.eater.com/2020/3/15/21180845/california-coronavirus-bars-restaurants-newsom.

64. Dave Goldiner and Chris Sommerfeldt, "Cuomo Cautions 'Fear and Panic Could Be Even Worse Than the Coronavirus, As Cases Soar Above 5,000 in New York," New York *Daily News*, published March 19, 2020, https://www.nydailynews.com/coronavirus/ny-coronavirus-cuomo-respirator-20200319-xuimmmxatjcnpnvhvntqkp6mle-story.html.

65. Cuomo, *American Crisis*, 104.

66. J. David Goodman, "How Delays and Unheeded Warnings Hindered New York's Virus Fight," the *New York Times*, published April 8, 2020, https://www.nytimes.com/2020/04/08/nyregion/new-york-coronavirus-response-delays.html.

67. "COVID-19 Projections: Delayed Response to Rebound Would Cost Lives," Columbia Mailman School of Public Health, published May 21, 2020, https://www.publichealth.columbia.edu/public-health-now/news/covid-19-projections-delayed-response-rebound-would-cost-lives?utm_source=Faculty+and+Staff+%28July+2018.

68. Jeffrey Shaman, in discussion with the author, December 22, 2020.

69. Ross Barkan, "New York's Transit Workers Keep Getting Sick," *The Nation*, published April 9, 2020, https://www.thenation.com/article/politics/mta-transit-driver-covid/.

70. Ebony Bowden, Carl Campanile, and Bruce Golding, "Worker at NYC Hospital Where Nurses Wear Trash Bags as Protection Dies from Coronavirus," *New York Post*, published March 25, 2020, https://nypost.com/2020/03/25/worker-at-nyc-hospital-where-nurses-wear-trash-bags-as-protection-dies-from-coronavirus/.

71. Joseph Goldstein, Michael Rothfeld, and Somini Sengupta, "13 Deaths in a Day: An 'Apocalyptic' Coronavirus Surge at an NYC Hospital," the *New York Times*, published March 25, 2020, https://www.nytimes.com/2020/03/25/nyregion/nyc-coronavirus-hospitals.html.

72. Anna Gustafson, "Hundreds Rally to Save Peninsula Hospital," *Queens Chronicle*, published August 25, 2011, https://www.qchron.com/editions/south/hundreds-rally-to-save-peninsula-hospital/article_9cc88d87-1be2-5a22-b35f-746e58ce6730.html.

73. David Brand, "'Overwhelmed' St John's Hospital in Far Rockaway Needs 30 Ventilators, Councilman Says," *Queens Daily Eagle*, published March 31, 2020, https://queenseagle.com/all/overwhelmed-st-johns-hospital-needs-30-ventilators-councilman-says.

74. Kassie Bracken and Emily Rhyne, "'Lord Have Mercy': Inside One of New York's Deadliest Zip Codes," the *New York Times*, published May 22, 2020, https://www.nytimes.com/video/us/100000007097093/coronavirus-st-johns-hospital-far-rockaway.html.

75. Christine Chung, Yoav Gonen, Clifford Michel, and Rachel Holliday Smith, "First Tally of Virus Death Toll by Neighborhood Shows City Split in Suffering," *The City,* published May 18, 2020, https://www.thecity.nyc/coronavirus/2020/5/18/21270843/first-tally-of-virus-death-toll-by-neighborhood-shows-city-split-in-suffering.

76. Guy Chazan, "Oversupply of Hospital Beds Helps Germany to Fight Virus," *Financial Times,* published April 12, 2020, https://www.ft.com/content/d979c0e9-4806-4852-a49a-bbffa9cecfe6.

77. Carl Campanile, Nolan Hicks, Bernadette Hogan, and Julia Marsh, "New York Has Thrown Away 20,000 Hospital Beds, Complicating Coronavirus Fight," *New York Post,* published March 17, 2020, https://nypost.com/2020/03/17/new-york-has-thrown-away-20000-hospital-beds-complicating-coronavirus-fight/.

78. "Our Vow: No More Closings," Official Website of the New York State Nurses Association, https://www.nysna.org/our-vow-no-more-closings.

79. Sara Dorn, "Coronavirus in NY: City's ICU-bed Capacity Ranks in Bottom Quarter Nationally," *New York Post,* published March 28, 2020, https://nypost.com/2020/03/28/coronavirus-in-ny-citys-icu-bed-capacity-ranks-in-bottom-quarter-nationally/.

80. Stephen Berger, "Why NYC Needs Hospitals to Close," *New York Post,* published September 9, 2013, https://nypost.com/2013/09/09/why-nyc-needs-hospitals-to-close/.

81. Ross Barkan, "Cuomo Helped Get New York Into This Mess," *The Nation,* published March 30, 2020, https://www.thenation.com/article/politics/covid-ny-hospital-medicaid/.

82. Ross Barkan, "How One Cozy Relationship Influenced Cuomo's Covid Response," *The Nation,* published March 12, 2021, https://www.thenation.com/article/society/cuomo-nursing-homes-campaign/

83. Katie Honan, Laura Kusisto, and Shalini Ramachandran, "How New York's Coronavirus Response Made the Pandemic Worse," *The Wall Street Journal,* published June 11, 2020, https://www.wsj.com/articles/how-new-yorks-coronavirus-response-made-the-pandemic-worse-11591908426.

84. Ross Barkan, "Cuomo Helped Get New York Into This Mess," *The Nation,* published March 30, 2020, https://www.thenation.com/article/politics/covid-ny-hospital-medicaid/.

85. Ross Barkan, "'Enough is Enough': Lawmakers Seek to Break Cuomo's Grip on NY's Budget," Gothamist, published April 26, 2019, https://gothamist.com/news/enough-is-enough-lawmakers-seek-to-break-cuomos-grip-on-nys-budget.

86. Anna Wilde Mathews, "New York Mandates Nursing Homes Take COVID-19 Patients Discharged From Hospitals," *The Wall Street Journal*, published March 26, 2020, https://www.wsj.com/articles/new-york-mandates-nursing-homes-take-covid-19-patients-discharged-from-hospitals-11585228215.

87. Samar Khurshid, "'Not a Budget Anybody Should Be Celebrating': Democratic Legislators Displeased with Albany Compromise," *Gotham Gazette*, published April 9, 2020, https://www.gothamgazette.com/state/9287-state-budget-dissent-democratic-legislators-albany-compromise-cuomo.

88. Ron Kim, in discussion with the author, December 30, 2020.

89. WRGB Staff, "Siena Poll: 84 Percent of New Yorkers Approve of Gov. Cuomo Amid Pandemic," WRBG Albany, published April 27, 2020, https://cbs6albany.com/news/local/siena-poll-84-of-new-yorkers-approve-of-gov-cuomo-amid-pandemic.

90. Mark Binelli, "Andrew Cuomo Takes Charge," *Rolling Stone*, published May 5, 2020, https://www.rollingstone.com/politics/politics-features/andrew-cuomo-new-york-coronavirus-982087/.

91. Jake Offenhartz, "With 'No Support' From the State, Patients Endure 'A Living Nightmare' in NY's Hardest Hit Nursing Home," Gothamist, published April 24, 2020, https://gothamist.com/news/no-support-state-patients-endure-living-nightmare-nys-hardest-hit-nursing-home.

92. J. David Goodman and William K. Rashbaum, "NYC Death Toll Soars Past 10,000 in Revised Virus Count," the *New York Times*, published April 14, 2020, https://www.nytimes.com/2020/04/14/nyregion/new-york-coronavirus-deaths.html.

93. Alex Rivera, in discussion with the author, July 24, 2020.

94. April Reese, in discussion with the author, July 24, 2020.

95. Brigida Bautista, in discussion with the author, July 24, 2020.

96. Reuven Blau, "Prisoners Hoping for Mercy Place Little Faith in Cuomo," *The City*, published December 22, 2020, https://www.thecity.nyc/2020/12/22/22196558/prisoners-hoping-for-mercy-place-little-faith-in-cuomo.

97. Jim Dwyer, "More Mercy, Less Prison in a Shift for Cuomo," published October 21, 2015, https://www.nytimes.com/2015/10/22/nyregion/more-mercy-less-prison-in-a-shift-for-albany.html.

98. "A State-by-State Look at Coronavirus in Prisons," The Marshall Project, updated February 26, 2021, https://www.themarshallproject.org/2020/05/01/a-state-by-state-look-at-coronavirus-in-prisons.

99. Chelsea Clinton, Twitter, published January 13, 2021, https://twitter.com/ChelseaClinton/status/1349409374448607235.

100. Troy Closson, "The High-Risk Group Left Out of New York's Vaccine Rollout," the *New York Times*, published January 26, 2021, https://www.nytimes.com/2021/01/26/nyregion/new-york-vaccine-prisons.html.

101. Rosa Goldensohn, "State Prison COVID-19 Wave Grows as Inmates Wait for Vaccines," *The City*, published January 18, 2021, https://www.thecity.nyc/2021/1/18/22237488/new-york-prison-covid-cases-grow-inmates-vaccines-cuomo.

102. "By 2-to-1, Voters Say Moving Too Quickly to Loosen Stay-at-Home Orders is Bigger Danger than Moving Too Slowly," Siena College Research Institute, published May 27, 2020, https://scri.siena.edu/2020/05/27/by-2-to-1-voters-say-moving-too-quickly-to-loosen-stay-at-home-orders-is-bigger-danger-than-moving-too-slowly/.

103. Robert Caro, *The Power Broker: Robert Moses and the Fall of New York*, (New York: Alfred A. Knopf, 1974) 633.

104. Zellnor Y. Myrie, Twitter, published July 13, 2020, https://twitter.com/zellnor4ny/status/1282869947643854849.

105. Nathan Layne and Jessica Resnick-Ault, "Coronavirus Came to New York from Europe, Not China—Governor," Reuters, published April 24, 2020, https://www.reuters.com/article/us-healthcare-coronavirus-usa-new-york/coronavirus-came-to-new-york-from-europe-not-china-governor-says-idUSKCN2262MQ.

106. Andrew Cuomo, Twitter, published March 22, 2020, https://twitter.com/NYGovCuomo/status/1241750717939007490.

107. Aaron Carr, "Cuomo's Density Dodge: Pandemics Aren't Anti-city, Failure to Act Early Is," *Gotham Gazette*, published April 28, 2020, https://www.gothamgazette.com/open-government/130-opinion/9342-cuomo-density-coronavirus-pandemics-anti-city-failure-act-early.

108. "Cuomo, De Blasio Announce Citywide Curfew After Peaceful George Floyd Protests Spiral into Chaos," CBS New York, published June 1, 2020, https://newyork.cbslocal.com/2020/06/01/nyc-possible-curfew-protests/.

109. Commissioner Margaret Garnett, "Investigation into NYPD Response to the George Floyd Protests," published December 18, 2020, https://www1.nyc.gov/assets/doi/reports/pdf/2020/DOIRpt.NYPD%20Reponse.%20GeorgeFloyd%20Protests.12.18.2020.pdf.

110. Ross Barkan, "Cuomo's Nursing Home Investigation May Present 'Conflict of Interest,'" Gothamist, published May 7, 2020, https://gothamist.com/news/cuomos-nursing-home-investigation-may-present-conflict-interest.

111. Ross Barkan, "Cuomo's Administration Faces Questioning Over Its Handling of Nursing Home COVID-19 Deaths," *The Nation*, published August 10, 2020, https://www.thenation.com/article/politics/cuomo-covid-nursing-homes/.

112. Bernard Condon, Meghan Hoyer, and Matt Sedensky, "New York's True Nursing Home Death Toll Cloaked in Secrecy," AP News, published August 10, 2020, https://apnews.com/article/ap-top-news-understanding-the-outbreak-new-york-andrew-cuomo-health-212ccd87924b6906053703a00514647f.

113. Jesse McKinley, Twitter, published January 28, 2021, https://twitter.com/jessemckinley/status/1354914653953007624.

114. Bill Hammond, "New York Reveals Another 1,516 COVID-19 Deaths in Long-Term Care Facilities," Empire Center for Public Policy, published February 7, 2021, https://www.empirecenter.org/publications/new-york-reveals-another-1516-covid-19-deaths-in-long-term-care-facilities/.

115. Carl Campanile, Bernadette Hogan, and Bruce Golding. "Cuomo Aide Melissa DeRosa Admits They Hid Nursing Home Data So Feds Wouldn't Find Out," *New York Post*, published February 11, 2021, https://nypost.com/2021/02/11/cuomo-aide-admits-they-hid-nursing-home-data-from-feds.

116. Gwynne Hogan and Christopher Robbins. "Cuomo Unleashed Tirade on Queens Lawmaker And Threatens to 'Destroy' Him After Nursing Home Deaths Criticism," Gothamist, published February 17, 2021, https://gothamist.com/news/cuomo-unleashes-tirade-on-queens-lawmaker-and-threatens-to-destroy-him-after-nursing-home-deaths-criticism.
117. "Spending by NYC on Charter School Facilities: Diverted Resources, Inequities, and Anomalies," Class Size Matters, published October 21, 2019, https://www.classsizematters.org/wp-content/uploads/2019/10/Charter-School-Facility-Costs-10.21.19.pdf.
118. Robert Harding, "NYSUT, NY's Powerful Teachers Union, Doesn't Endorse Cuomo or Asotrino in Race for Governor," The Citizen, published August 15, 2014, https://auburnpub.com/blogs/eye_on_ny/nysut-nys-powerful-teachers-union-doesnt-endorse-cuomo-or-astorino-in-race-for-governor/article_a777410c-23b7-11e4-8f2f-001a4bcf887a.html.
119. Anya Kamenetz, "NYC Teachers Union 'Prepared to Strike' If Safety Demands Are Not Met," NPR, published August 19, 2020, https://www.npr.org/sections/coronavirus-live-updates/2020/08/19/903927057/nyc-teacher-unions-prepared-to-strike-if-safety-demands-are-not-met.
120. J. David Goodman and Dana Rubenstein, "Suprising Results in Initial Virus Testing in NYC Schools," the New York Times, published October 19, 2020, https://www.nytimes.com/2020/10/19/nyregion/schools-coronavirus.html.
121. Nancy Cutler, "Cuomo Team Uses 2006 Photo of Satmar Rabbi's Funeral to Illustrate 'Super-spreader' Events," The Journal News, published October 5, 2020, https://www.lohud.com/story/news/local/rockland/2020/10/05/cuomo-2006-photo-rabbi-funeral-coronavirus/3621444001/.
122. "Joint Statement from Senator Simcha Felder, Assemblyman Simcha Eichenstein, Councilman Chaim Deutsch, and Councilman Kalman Yeger," Hamodia, published October 6, 2020, https://hamodia.com/2020/10/06/joint-statement-senator-simcha-felder-assemblyman-simcha-eichenstein-councilman-chaim-deutsch-counsilman-kalman-yeger/.

123. Leia Idliby, "Cuomo Brutally Scolds a Reporter and Insists NYC Schools Won't Be Closed, Minutes Before Announcement Schools Will Be Closed," Mediaite, published November 18, 2020, https://www.mediaite.com/tv/watch-cuomo-brutally-scolds-a-reporter-and-insists-nyc-schools-wont-be-closed-minutes-before-announcement-schools-will-be-closed/.

124. The Recount, Twitter, published November 18, 2020, https://twitter.com/therecount/status/1329174340806602753.

125. Roger Starr, "Making New York Smaller," the *New York Times*, Published November 14, 1976, https://www.nytimes.com/1976/11/14/archives/making-new-york-smaller-the-citys-economic-outlook-remains-grim.html.

126. Cuomo, *American Crisis*, 10.

127. Sam Roberts, "Jerry Birbach, Leader of Fight to Block Poor Tenants in Queens, Dies at 87," the *New York Times*, published March 1, 2017, https://www.nytimes.com/2017/03/01/nyregion/jerry-birbach-dead-led-forest-hills-protest.html.

128. Andrew Cuomo, *All Things Possible: Setbacks and Success in Politics and Life*, (New York: HarperCollins, 2014) 47.

129. Daniel L. Feldman, "Koch and Cuomo," Tales From the Sausage Factory, published November 18, 2011, https://talesfromthesausagefactory.wordpress.com/2011/11/18/koch-and-cuomo/.

130. James Dao, "In Message, Cuomo Echoes GOP Ideas," the *New York Times*, published January 6, 1994, https://www.nytimes.com/1994/01/06/nyregion/in-message-cuomo-echoes-gop-ideas.html.

131. Frank Lynn, "Cuomo Hoards His $5 Million Fund," the *New York Times*, published October 27, 1990, https://www.nytimes.com/1990/10/27/nyregion/cuomo-hoards-his-5-million-fund.html.

132. Sam Howe Verhovek, "The 1992 Election: New York State—The New York Legislature; Once Again, Republicans Maintain Control of the Senate," published November 4, 1992, https://www.nytimes.com/1992/11/04/nyregion/1992-election-new-york-state-new-york-legislature-once-again-republicans.html.

133. Cuomo, *All Things Possible*, 196.

134. Cuomo, *All Things Possible*, 198.

135. Cuomo, *All Things Possible*, 145.

136. Nicholas Confessore, "Cuomo Vows Offensive Against Labor Unions," the *New York Times*, published October 24, 20120, https://www.nytimes.com/2010/10/25/nyregion/25cuomo.html.

137. Thomas Kaplan, "Cuomo Rejects Another Plan by De Blasio: Minimum Wage," the *New York Times*, published February 11, 2014, https://www.nytimes.com/2014/02/12/nyregion/cuomo-rejects-another-plan-by-de-blasio-minimum-wage.html.

138. Cuomo, *All Things Possible*, 271–272.

139. Tom Precious, "As Innermost Adviser to Cuomo Since 90s, Joe Percoco Was Family's 'Third Son,'" *The Buffalo News*, published September 28, 2016, https://buffalonews.com/news/local/govt-and-politics/as-innermost-adviser-to-cuomo-since-90s-joe-percoco-was-family-s-third-son/article_990a83a0-a172-5e88-ab6d-18baed8bb7fe.html.

140. Ross Barkan, "Cuomo Silent on Taxing Ultrawealthy While Pushing Billions of Cuts to Localities," Gothamist, published April 29, 2020, https://gothamist.com/news/cuomo-silent-taxing-ultrawealthy-while-pushing-billions-cuts-localities.

141. Daniel Moritz-Rabson, "As Bills Pile Up, Getting Unemployment Benefits in NY a 'Kafkaesque Mess,'" Gothamist, published April 22, 2020, https://gothamist.com/news/coronavirus-unemployment-benefits-in-ny-is-still-a-kafkaesque-mess.

142. Janaki Chadha and Bill Mahoney, "New York Lawmakers Approve Sweeping Eviction Moratorium," *Politico*, published December 28, 2020, https://www.politico.com/states/new-york/albany/story/2020/12/28/new-york-lawmakers-approve-sweeping-eviction-moratorium-1351393.

143. Cezary Podkul and Marcelo Rochabrun, "The Fateful Vote That Made New York City Rents So High," ProPublica, published December 15, 2016, https://www.propublica.org/article/the-vote-that-made-new-york-city-rents-so-high.

144. Georgia Kromrei, "Government for Sale," *The Indypendent*, published August 13, 2018, https://indypendent.org/2018/08/government-for-sale/.

145. Blake Zeff, "Another Cuomo Noninterference Story Falls Apart," *Politico*, published September 2, 2014, https://www.politico.com/states/new-york/albany/story/2016/05/another-cuomo-noninterference-story-falls-apart-049022.

146. Steven Wishnia, "'When It Rains Outside, It Rains Inside': Tenants Say Notorious NYC Landlord Is Practicing 'Construction as Harassment,'" *The Village Voice*, published December 20, 2016, https://www.villagevoice.com/2016/12/20/when-it-rains-outside-it-rains-inside-tenants-say-notorious-nyc-landlord-is-practicing-construction-as-harassment/.

147. Michael McKee, in discussion with the author, January 25, 2021.

148. Jazmine Hughes and Dana Rubinstein, "New York Halted Evictions. But What Happens When the Ban Ends?," the *New York Times*, published January 1, 2021, https://www.nytimes.com/2021/01/01/nyregion/nyc-eviction-moratorium-shelters.html.

149. insert text

150. Ross Barkan, "Cuomo's Budget Strategy: A Long Game of Chicken with Donald Trump," Gothamist, published June 29, 2020, https://gothamist.com/news/cuomos-budget-strategy-a-long-game-of-chicken-with-donald-trump.

151. Carl Campanile, "Cuomo Announces Income Tax Revenues Have Dropped by $2.3 Billion," *The New York Post*, published February 4, 2019, https://nypost.com/2019/02/04/cuomo-announces-income-tax-revenues-have-dropped-by-2-3b/.

152. Ross Barkan, "If Cuomo Cuts Funding, CUNY Layoffs Will Be a 'Bloodbath,'" *The Nation*, published May 20, 2020, https://www.thenation.com/article/society/new-york-cuomo-cuny-cuts/.

153. Ross Barkan, "CUNY Grapples with Devastating Budget Cuts: 'People Are Freaking Out or Getting Fired,'" Gothamist, published October 15, 2020, https://gothamist.com/news/cuny-grapples-with-devastating-budget-cuts-people-are-freaking-out-or-getting-fired.

154. "Twenty Watchdog Groups Call for State Budget Withholding Transparency," Reinvent Albany, published December 22, 2020, https://reinventalbany.org/2020/12/twenty-watchdog-groups-call-for-state-budget-withholding-transparency/.

155. Angela Butel and James Parrott, "New York State's Historic Divestment in Human Services since the Great Recession," The Center for New York City Affairs at The New School, published March 2019, http://www.centernyc.org/ny-state-historic-disinvestment.

156. Joseph Goldstein, "Virus Numbers Are Surging. Why Is New York's Vaccine Rollout Sluggish?," the *New York Times*, published January 1, 2021, https://www.nytimes.com/2021/01/01/nyregion/nyc-covid-vaccine-rollout.html.

157. Neil Postman, *Amusing Ourselves to Death: Public Discourse in the Age of Show Business*, (New York: Viking Penguin, 1985) 159.

158. David Wallace-Wells, "Governor Covid: Andrew Cuomo Tries to Makes Sense of the Last Seven Months," *New York Magazine*, published October 11, 2020.

ABOUT THE AUTHOR

Ross Barkan is the author of five books, including the novel *Glass Century*. He's a contributing writer to the *NY Times Magazine*, a columnist for *NY Magazine*, and the editor-in-chief of *The Metropolitan Review*, a books and culture review publication.

www.ingramcontent.com/pod-product-compliance
Lightning Source LLC
Jackson TN
JSHW022227050525
83811JS00002B/3